PERFECTLY WOUNDED

PERFECTLY WOUNDED

A MEMOIR ABOUT WHAT HAPPENS AFTER A MIRACLE

MIKE DAY

with Robert Vera

TWELVE

NEW YORK

Copyright © 2020 by Douglas Michael Day
Photographs courtesy of the author
Map by Jeffrey L. Ward
Jacket copyright © 2020 by Hachette Book Group, Inc.

Twelve
Hachette Book Group
1290 Avenue of the Americas, New York, NY 10104
twelvebooks.com
twitter.com/twelvebooks

First Edition: June 2020

Twelve is an imprint of Grand Central Publishing. The Twelve name and logo are trademarks of Hachette Book Group, Inc.

The publisher is not responsible for websites (or their content) that are not owned by the publisher.

The Hachette Speakers Bureau provides a wide range of authors for speaking events. To find out more, go to www.hachettespeakersbureau.com or call (866) 376-6591.

LCCN: 2020931755

ISBNs: 978-1-5387-0183-6 (hardcover), 978-1-5387-0182-9 (ebook)

Printed in the United States of America

LSC-C

10 9 8 7 6 5 4 3 2 1

To the beaten souls that continue to thrive, and the innocent souls about to begin the journey.

Contents

Author's Note   ix

Foreword by Adm. William H. McRaven   xi

Preface by Lt. Chris Tyll, Navy SEAL   xv

Map   xix

Part I
TESTED

1: SEAL Team 4, Foxtrot Platoon   3

2: God Get Me Home   15

3: Resiliency Training   31

4: Boot Camp to BUD/S   43

5: SEAL Team 3—Surf Reports   71

6: Leap Frogs   81

7: Kosovo, Body Parts, and Danger Close   91

8: September 11, 2001   95

9: Ambushes and Miniguns   99

Part II
TRANSFORMED

10: Medevac   105

11: Baghdad to Germany to Home   113

12: Perfectly Wounded   121

Part III
AWAKE

13: The Enemy Within   137

14: Case Fixer vs. Case Manager   139

15: Climbing Mountains   153

16: Breakthrough and Breakdown   161

17: Ironmans and Hollywood   171

18: The Right Relationships   181

19: New Thoughts, New Job, New Life   191

20: Tattoos   199

21: Personal Revolution: Resiliency Skills and Tools   203

EPILOGUE: Joseph Clark Schwedler   209

ACKNOWLEDGMENTS   211

ABOUT THE AUTHORS   213

Author's Note

The events in this book are all true.

Parts of my story have been retold publicly by third parties in books, in the Hollywood film *Act of Valor*, and in various media reports. Prior to the release of these books, media reports, and film, I was never consulted, nor did I provide any details about my story to any of these third-party reports. The complete firsthand account of what happened to me and my SEAL platoon on April 6 and 7, 2007, and the events before and after that time, have never been released until now. I have constructed the dialogue from various sources, including my own memory. Thus, the dialogue may not be exactly word for word; however, the meaning of what was said is accurate. Lastly, for security reasons I have changed the names of many of the key people and places in this story.

Foreword

If you're really lucky in life, you will have an opportunity to meet someone like Mike Day. Someone who has overcome so many challenges, whose spirit seems unbreakable, whose heroism is matched only by their humility and whose compassion for their fellow warriors knows no limits.

I first met Mike in 1994, when I was the new commanding officer of SEAL Team 3 in Coronado, California. Every morning the entire team would muster for physical training (PT) on the grinder, a large patch of asphalt behind the headquarters building. Gathering in a circle, we would do our calisthenics for an hour and then go for a long run or tackle a grueling obstacle course. But the daily ritual on the grinder was much more than just doing PT. It was where the team came together to test one another—to find one another's weaknesses and exploit them to the amusement of everyone else. It was a full-on, testosterone-raging alpha-male harassment session that left no one unscathed, including the commanding officer. It was also the place where I could measure the morale of the team. It was where you quickly assessed who were the leaders in the command and who were the followers—who was respected and who was left wanting.

It didn't take me long to see that Mike Day was one of the leaders, and, even though quite junior at the time, he was highly respected by his fellow SEALs. Mike had a wicked sense of humor and a quick wit that he used to great effect on the other members of the team. But he was equally self-effacing and was more often to be the butt of his own jokes. Mike was the guy you wanted in your SEAL platoon. He always had a smile on his face, always laughing about something. Always willing to help. And always taking the jobs no one else wanted. He was the perfect SEAL swim buddy.

Mike eventually transferred to the Navy parachute team, and, just as he was regarded during his time at SEAL Team Three, he was universally liked and respected by the other SEALs. As I moved on and Mike transferred to another command, I lost track of him.

Fifteen years later, as I stood outside the Intensive Care Unit at the military hospital in Landsthul, Germany, I wondered how much Mike Day might have changed. He had just been AIR-EVACed from Iraq after having been shot twenty-seven times by al-Qaida fighters. As I walked into his room, struggling with what I might say to a man so badly injured, I heard Mike yell from his bedside, "Hey, Skipper! What the hell are you doing here?" A big smile came across his face, then he laughed and motioned me to his bedside. Looking down at his body, I was stunned at what I saw. Hardly an inch of his flesh wasn't covered with bullet holes. In all my years of talking to wounded soldiers in the ICU, I had never seen anyone so badly shot up. He was as animated as always—harassing me about our time at SEAL Team Three and laughing about his current situation. I knew that morphine and life-saving drugs were pulsing through his veins and I guessed that he would never remember our conversation. He soon fell back to sleep, and I left him to rest.

Mike returned to the States and, over the years, I watched

as he recovered from his wounds. Little did I know at the time that Mike's trauma went much deeper than just the bullet holes in his body.

Perfectly Wounded is a raw, uncensored look at one man's survival from a childhood of pain and unspeakable horrors to a life of service, a legacy of remarkable courage and unwavering commitment, and, above all, duty to others. Mike Day's life will not be defined by his wounds, seen or unseen, but by how he coped with their aftermath. It will not be defined by that fateful day in Iraq, but by the life that followed and countless wounded warriors he helped. This book is for every man and woman who struggles in life and is looking for how best to overcome the challenges with dignity, honor, and compassion. This book is for everyone.

Admiral William H. McRaven

(U.S. Navy, Retired)

Preface

Recollections from Lt. Chris Tyll, Navy SEAL

I was a newly minted Navy SEAL officer when I arrived in Iraq and met Mike Day. He was the chief, the senior enlisted guy in Foxtrot platoon. I was assigned to Echo, our sister platoon. Chief Day was hard, even by Navy SEAL standards, and repetition was his brand: he would have us all do ball-busting training over and over again, and just when you thought you were done for the day, he would say, "Let's do it again."

It would be a big mistake to believe that Chief Day was not prepared for anything; to him, that mind-set seemed amateurish. Mike Day was prepared for everything, and he was going to be absolutely sure that you were prepared too. While others trained hard, Chief Day worked at a different level. He made us all raise our game, and he did so not with orders or yelling—it was far worse than that. He did it by example. This "old man" of thirty-eight years was out there grinding with all the young Navy SEAL studs; he was up at the front and he was pushing everyone far beyond their breaking points. Don't misunderstand me—he did yell, but rarely, and only when you pissed him off, usually because you did something stupid. Then his blue eyes would light up like lasers and lock on their target, and then he'd tear into you. Everything stopped; there was silence, except for Chief Day, who seemed to be yelling at a frequency that shut out all other sounds, because we could all hear him loud and clear. A Chief Day berating was impactful because he was impactful; in that moment when he was a few feet from your face, there was nobody who could have been more influential than Mike Day. Not the president of the United States, not the secretary of defense, not even an admiral. Mike Day's authority and credibility far exceeded his rank. He may not have known it, but we all did.

Of all my time in the military, I can say that Mike Day's SEAL platoon was the best group of guys I ever worked with. They were total professionals, with a work ethic that was second to none. We had highly educated guys who could run, swim, and fight. They were all professional warfighters. The guys Mike Day trained with would later be assigned to other teams, and all of them would better their new teams with their presence. They would take care of their teammates just like Mike took care of us. They would stack up awards, and one would later earn the military's highest recognition: the Medal of Honor. I believe Mike did it because he loved us—we were his "other" family. What he wanted most was for all of his teammates to get home—that's why he hammered us. He was preparing us to face the demons that he already knew too well. After his war ended, his wounds not yet fully healed, he went straight back into the fight, taking care of his fellow warriors and their families as a case manager at the Special Operations Command (SOCOM) Care Coalition. He would battle the bureaucracy at the Veterans Administration and other agencies to ensure his fellow warriors received the best possible care. When Mike Day entered the fight, the odds changed, because he was willing and able to out-suffer, outfight, and outlast everyone. Even this story is Mike's attempt to honor and care for others. Mike Day's survival and his entire story are beyond belief—his experience and being with him during it marked a turning point in my own life.

In the Navy SEAL community, Mike Day is a legend, a giant who walks among giants.

THE SUNNI TRIANGLE, IRAQ

SYRIA

Tigris River

IRAN

Euphrates River

Tikrit

Habbaniyah Lake

Ramadi

Fallujah

Baghdad

BAGHDAD
INTERNATIONAL
AIRPORT

Razazza Lake

Tigris River

IRAQ

Euphrates River

SAUDI ARABIA

0 Miles   50   100

0 Kilometers   100

© 2020 Jeffrey L. Ward

Part I

TESTED

There is no normal life that is free of pain. It's the very wrestling with our problems that can be the impetus for our growth.

—Fred Rogers,
*The World According
to Mister Rogers*

CHAPTER 1

SEAL Team 4, Foxtrot Platoon

Modern warfare is impersonal and fought over long distances. Pilots who drop bombs and shoot guns from their aircraft seldom see their enemies up close. It's a rare event when combatants fight each other so near that you can smell your enemy's body odor. I have seen my enemies up close, in small rooms; I have seen their faces as we each did our best to kill each other. I have seen their final expressions frozen in time after bullets from my weapon struck their bodies.

I had been a Navy SEAL (Sea, Air, and Land) for nearly eighteen years when I arrived in Iraq in October 2006. I had already been on hundreds of missions with various SEAL platoons. This last platoon, SEAL Team 4, Foxtrot, was the best I'd ever worked with: a serious, disciplined, and highly skilled group of SEALs, all of us in great shape. We were at the top of the warrior food chain. Together we were lethal. We moved, communicated, and shot with the flawless precision of a symphony orchestra. We were a lethal war-fighting organism able to seek out, capture, and destroy the enemy, anywhere.

Second Iraq Deployment—SEAL Team 4, 3 Troop, Foxtrot Platoon

As a chief, and a senior guy on the team, one of my main responsibilities was to schedule, track, and coordinate our team's predeployment work-ups. This process took about eighteen months. It's broken into three phases and starts with a list of specific requirements of all the skills and equipment needed to deploy in order to follow through on our assignment. Not many people outside the SEAL community understand the volume and intensity of training that every SEAL undergoes during his career. BUD/S (Basic Underwater Demolition/SEAL) training is very basic—it's the lowest possible hurdle to cross to get onto the teams. Being a SEAL is a never-ending education. You are either fighting or training to fight.

This is where real training starts. There are three specific new layers of pre-deployment training. The first is professional development, then Unit Level Training, and finally Task Group Training. My role was to make sure all our guys were individually trained and cross-trained in various skill sets. Breachers, snipers, medics, drivers, radio operators, drone pilots, or whatever else the mission called for: I made sure our guys had the training. After everyone qualified and returned from training, I helped coordinate the six-month block of Unit Level Training and then the final six-month block of Task Group Training, where we brought everyone together to practice with all of the various pieces of the puzzle in place. Once all the training was complete, we loaded up and flew to Iraq to go to war.

Camp Fallujah, Iraq

There are very few times in life when the right group of people all meet at the right time. Most will never experience how it feels to be part of a team with exceptional people who are fully committed to each other and the mission. In all my years in the Navy, of all the platoons I've been a part of, SEAL Team 4, Foxtrot platoon was the best platoon I got to work with, hands down. The leadership was shrewd, mission-focused, and worked like animals alongside all the guys.

Our young SEALs—Clarkie, Micky, Jamie, and the others—were excellent operators, already seasoned well beyond their years. We had other guys assigned to us who were practically wizards—like Davidson, a Navy communications tech. This kid could make crazy sophisticated electronic tools using stuff like a broomstick and a piece of wire. He used his skills and tools to guide us through mazes of streets and alleys in the pitch dark, placing us directly on our targets within 95 percent accuracy.

When I arrived in Fallujah, the very first thing I did was figure out who owned the battle space. There is a process to war that includes extensive coordination and deconfliction between forces. We are all professional warfighters and as such we don't just start driving around a war zone shooting off weapons. Iraq was broken up into big chunks, and different branches of the U.S. military controlled different areas. Our district of Fallujah was run by the Marines. I was rummaging through some papers in our command shed looking for a list of contacts for the various commands on our base when I came across an old two-page phone list stuffed in a plastic sleeve. War includes constant turnover of people, units, and commands. It requires constant communication and relationship building to keep current with everything happening in the battle space. I started making calls attempting to learn who was in control of our sector. Most of the numbers didn't work, but I kept dialing, crossing them off as I went down the list. Finally, I dialed one that connected me to a Marine Corps colonel's office. Bingo! I explained who I was and that my team was new in town and was here to support them. The colonel welcomed the help and provided details on how to get missions submitted and approved.

While marines and soldiers patrolled the streets during the day, the SEALs used a sophisticated system to develop and cross-check specific targets. We would get approval to go after high-value targets late at night to either capture or kill them. In most cases, we captured targets because they would give us more useful intel, and most were Sunni. Many of these detainees would offer us valuable intel if we promised not to turn them over to our Iraqi colleagues, most of whom were Shia and many of whose families had been murdered by Sunnis.

Iraq's Al Anbar Province was Sunni turf: the Sunnis didn't like us, as they believed we were allied with their Shia enemy. I guess I can understand why, as nearly all our Iraqi army scouts were Shia. The younger guys in Foxtrot seemed to understand that this was a critical time in history.

I remember the first day training our group of fifty new Iraqi army recruits. I asked them to do ten push-ups—and most of them quit in protest, reducing our group of fifty to ten in under a minute. We trained up the ones who stayed and took pretty good care of them.

We were operating in Fallujah, a city in the heart of the Sunni Triangle. The triangle is a densely populated region of

Iraq inhabited mostly by Sunni Muslims that spans more than 2,700 miles, with boundaries extending from the densely populated cities of Baghdad to the east, Ramadi to the west, and Tikrit to the north. Fallujah, located about halfway between Baghdad and Ramadi, had recently seen an influx of Sunni foreign fighters and insurgents. These groups would launch attacks on us, Iraqi police stations, and on other targets under the cover of the local Sunni population. We didn't care much about the Sunni–Shia scrap; we just wanted to get in, do the work, and get out.

Iraq was full of bad guys controlling different parts of the country. The military intelligence community came up with decks of cards containing the faces of the most wanted terrorists in each region. It was like a baseball card collection of evil players, ranked based on their priority of capture. We hunted for the fifty-two most wanted bad guys in Al Anbar Province. When we arrived in country, there were forty-eight still at large; four of them had been captured or killed before we got there. It took a couple weeks to figure out the Marines' mission-approval process. The Marines had a different set of procedures for mission write-up requests: we once had a mission request denied because I used the wrong font in my PowerPoint. I'm sure that there were lots of good reasons for using a particular font, but I was not privy to any of them. I changed the font and the mission was approved.

The Marines are locked down, they are always good to go, they shoot straight, are excellent war fighters, and are disciplined. It was great working side by side with them. They take immense pride in everything that they do, including conditioning and appearance. Their officers would get upset with us for coming into their chow hall all dirty and bloody the morning after our night ops. War is already extremely stressful, and countless rules, regulations, and demands can add to the stress. From our standpoint, it seemed inconsequential that we walked into the chow hall hungry and tired in our dirty clothes after eight hours of risking our lives hunting and killing bad guys. However, from the Marines' point of view, orders were orders, and it was not about our dirty uniforms—they didn't want us setting a precedent and influencing their young marines. I had to continually balance this tension to defuse the stress. I'm more of a "creative thinker," and while I always acknowledged the rules, I interpreted them a little differently, depending on the situation. It was fortunate that I landed in the Navy and the SEAL teams; they gave me just enough latitude to develop my leadership skills.

Early on in the deployment, we snatched up three or four bad guys and were driving back to the base with our cargo. It was well past the 11:00 p.m. curfew, and we were using our night-vision goggles instead of headlights to see. Our six vehicles were blacked out and moving fast down a narrow road when we rolled up on three guys armed with AK-47s strapped to their backs. That's how the enemy operated most of the time—in three-man cells. One guy would plant the bomb while the other two acted as lookouts. One of the guys was planting an IED (improvised explosive device) in the road about twenty feet ahead of us. His two buddies bolted when they saw us, almost too late. They ran down an alley between some houses and melted back into the fabric of Fallujah. I let our 50-gunner open up on the remaining enemy IED planter. Our guy shot four rounds from his M2 Browning .50 caliber belt-fed machine gun. Every fourth round in the belt was a Raufoss Mk 211 multi-purpose high-explosive incendiary round. This sucker packs a punch and will drill through tank armor. The fourth round hit the guy in the upper right leg and blew it clean off. I watched his leg fly off his body and cartwheel in the air. I didn't see exactly where it landed, but it was far from where it came off. I decided that it was best to get us out of the area as fast as possible, but I do believe we neutralized that IED tech.

Our tempo was nearly nonstop. We only had time to go on missions, eat, try to get some sleep, and work out. It was a rare occasion when we had the time to "entertain" guests. We had one United Service Organizations (USO) celebrity visitor: the one and only Chuck Norris. Our higher-ups told us he was coming, and on the day of, he never showed. We all gave up and went to bed. I noticed that someone had written *Chuck Norris was here* in the portable toilet outside the chow hall. The *Chuck Norris was here* phrase is popular graffiti in dive bars, bathroom stalls, and elsewhere Chuck Norris has never been.

The next morning, someone came to wake me up and let me know that Chuck Norris was waiting in our team ready room. I was the first to arrive. I shook his hand and said, "You're late." We chatted for a few minutes; then I asked him if he had recently visited the toilet near the chow hall. He said no. When the other guys arrived, we took pictures, told some war stories, and he wrote *Chuck Norris was here* on our team room wall. He is a great guy and patriot, and he looked in great shape for a dude in his sixties. We all appreciated him visiting. The man is the epitome of "badass." The guys I worked with actually embodied Chuck's persona more than the man himself did.

An Army general also paid us a visit and gave us kudos for our work. Then he said, "If there's anything you guys need, let me know."

I raised my hand. "Yes, sir, we really could use some mini-guns and a few RG-31s." I remembered from my first deployment to Iraq how effective a minigun was and thought it would be a good idea to have a few now, just in case. And the RG-31 is a V-hull-shaped multipurpose IED-resistant beast of a vehicle. I saw one take an IED blast that would have made mulch out of our Humvees, and the RG-31 and all its occupants survived. I guess the general's statement was more rhetorical, though, because everyone turned and looked at me, kind of stunned, and the general didn't respond. I was totally serious—if I ever need to go back to war, it will be in an RG-31 with a few miniguns.

We had a very strong working relationship with our young Iraqi scouts. This was partly due to money. When we learned that our scouts were having problems getting paid, we took it upon ourselves to have a private chat with their commander to help clear up his confusion. After our informal "audit," their payroll glitch was fixed. From that point forward, our Iraqi trainees trusted us more than their own command. In my experience, effective leadership is not about telling people what to do, or using people to achieve your own personal goals; this type of leadership backfires and people will either leave, find a way to leave, or do the opposite of what they are asked to do until they leave. I have come to learn that the most effective leaders build trust and legitimacy with everyone around them.

This is what our platoon did with our new Iraqi scouts. We spent hours training them. When we saw the condition of their barracks, the boys rallied together and helped the scouts do some much-needed renovations. Our platoon would hang out with them and drink tea. It was not forced: we took care of them because we cared about them. In their eyes, we became legitimate allies. Trust builds legitimacy, and trust is the currency of every effective leader. I could see the changes—over the course of a few months, these guys, who could have once been our enemies, trusted and liked us. Our young Iraqi scouts began emulating our guys, wearing wraparound sunglasses and their ball caps backward like we did. They came up with a unit name—Scorpions—and their own patch. It was cool. I wore their Iraqi flag on one arm and an American flag on the other; they loved it. Before we could lead, help, or teach them, they needed to trust us. They needed to feel safe with us. Trust and leadership work the same way in every workplace. However, I have come to learn that the most unfortunate part about trust is that some people in charge don't realize that people don't trust them.

12:10 AM

One night we received intel that guy number four in our Deck of Cards had been spotted. We told the guys to saddle up, then Jack and I drove across the base to spin up our Iraqi trainees. We all loaded into two choppers and took off after Number Four. It was a fifteen-minute flight to the target, and Davidson had us locked on to the location. We put down close to the house, the choppers doing a touch-and-go, and twenty of us bolted out and took up positions around the house. It was pitch-dark, and once the choppers departed, the only sounds were a few barking dogs.

I found a door, cracked it open, and peeked in. There were seven men all sleeping on floor mats. Some had their AKs beside them; others had the barrels of their guns resting on their leg or stomach. There were dogs barking and helicopters flying, and I could not believe that they were still sound asleep. I whispered into my radio, "Two guys on each one of them, then we'll wake them up." We filed in the room and set up over each one of the snoozers. One of our guys at the head, another at the feet, weapons ready.

We would wake them all simultaneously with a tap on the head. "On my barrel nod, wake 'em up," I whispered.

CLONK. I poked my sleeping terrorist in the forehead with the tip of my M4 rifle. He was stunned; it took him a few seconds to realize he was awake and that I was now his living nightmare. He also knew that his career as a terrorist had abruptly ended; he was caught red-handed with his band of narcoleptic thugs. I would place their ages between nineteen and thirty; some of them were crying. But our target, the Number Four bad guy in Al Anbar, was not among them. We quickly learned his possible location after a couple brief discussions with his buddies. We cuffed our cargo and marched through the village to where they said our Deck of Cards target was held up. All of us just walked down the road under the glowing yellow streetlights while wild packs of dogs barked at us. That's the odd thing about humans—we become desensitized to the familiar. I learned in Iraq that if we tried to shoot out streetlights or quiet the barking dogs, it would wake people up. Uncommon distractions, not familiar ones, are what alert humans.

We walked right to the front door. Once there, we set up security, opened the door, walked in, and there he was, sound asleep—the fourth-most-wanted guy in the Deck of Cards. He reeked of stale cigarettes, BO, and some cheap cologne he probably thought covered up his stench. We snatched him up, secured the area, and called in the birds for extraction. We quickly stuffed everyone into two choppers and took off. I'm not sure what happened to any of our detainees from that operation.

We had been in Fallujah for nearly six months and would end up conducting a total of 140 direct-action missions. In the first four months of the deployment, Clarkie, Micky, and Jamie would frequently ask, "Hey, Chief, we got anything going on tonight?" They were bangry—half bored, half angry. Guys like us would much rather be shot at than suffer boredom. We SEALs are all so alike. I wanted to quit Navy boot camp on a daily basis because of the mind-numbing boredom. If you are fortunate enough to have a long military career, it will condition you to accept all kinds of dullness, to the point where you end up finding other productive things to do while you're hurrying up and waiting.

Target development is an iterative process. Over the course of the deployment, we worked hard to build a highly productive intelligence pipeline. We would gain useful information from our detainees. Some of our most productive information came about by simply asking "why": Why did you plant the bomb? Why did you help the bad guys? We would use the information to gain an understanding of each detainee's motivation. Our goal was to get the money men, the funders of insurgents, the kingpins and/or their kill teams. We would feed this and other information into a decision matrix to develop a set of new targets. Once a target was identified, we would create a mission to capture or kill our intended bad guys. We would then forward this plan to our command. Included with this plan were several options as to how we would go about executing the mission. After many layers of command evaluation, our plan would eventually be approved or denied. If accepted, the plan became a CONOP, or concept of operation; at that point all it needed was a trigger to be pulled and we loaded up and launched. A trigger is accurate and timely information on the specific location of our intended target. This entire process of identifying targets, building a network of "triggers," and establishing relationships with other organizations—including the Marines, Army, Air Force, Iraqi police, and the civilian population—all required restraint, consistency, and trust. The most important in this trinity was trust. We were constantly developing new targets and had ten to fifteen preapproved; we just had to wait for one of our kingpins to pop up on the radar.

The pace became so feverish, some of the guys came to me to ask if we were intentionally doing missions to drive up the operation numbers. We weren't—that's not how our war worked. Every mission had a specific target, and that target had to be in a known location at night for us to move. Daylight patrols and missions in a city full of enemies was dangerous, hot, hard work. The Army and Marines shouldered this thankless task admirably.

War is fickle. The more potshots and IEDs that miss you and injure or kill someone else, the more you believe it's only a matter of time before the roulette wheel of war stops on your number. I felt it but put it out of my mind and kept grinding away.

CHAPTER 2

God Get Me Home

Naval Special Warfare, Task Unit Fallujah April 2007, Al Anbar Province, Iraq

It was pitch dark when our Foxtrot platoon rolled out of the compound. The road leading us into the target was narrow, a dusty single-lane track. That road was our only way in and our only way out from the target. Jack and I sat up front in the lead Humvee, while five other Humvees tailed us. Clark "Clarkie" Schwedler—one of our go-to guys, who excelled at everything from navigation to shooting—brought up the rear, in the vehicle manning the 50-caliber machine gun.

We rumbled through the farming district with few homes and no streetlights. A few miles from our target, a blast shook the ground and rattled our Humvees. Clarkie and his crew had been hit by an IED. I'm not sure if they rolled over it or if it had been remotely detonated. There was no time to stop and figure it out, too risky. We sped through the area to a safe location, rallied up, and took inventory of personnel and equipment. The blast had rocked Clarkie's Humvee and rang a few bells, but there were no serious injuries. We called off the operation and returned to base to come up with an alternative plan.

IEDs were a constant hazard. I experienced a total of six IED blasts on this deployment alone. We had a convoy hit while transporting guys to the airport to catch their flight home. One of our guys—who had made it through the entire deployment without a scratch—earned a Purple Heart on his ride to the airport to fly out of Iraq that day. We were hit twice on this ride. One blast was in Fallujah just before crossing the bridge from which U.S. contractors were hanged and burned during an attack in March 2004. The event made headlines across the globe. One of the contractors, Scott Helvenston, was one of my BUD/S instructors. The second blast happened a couple miles down the road in a rural area. The IED ripped through the vehicle and a piece of fragmentation slipped in between the gunner's body armor. He was medevaced to Baghdad and came back to work a couple weeks later.

This was to be one of our last missions before rotating home. We were already in the process of bringing guys in from SEAL Team 10 and shipping out our guys from SEAL Team 4.

In less than two weeks, our entire team would rotate back to the United States. I knew that this mission was imminent, as our target was a hardcore al-Qaida terrorist who led an effective cell of fighters. This particular terrorist group had shot down four of our medevac helicopters, killing everyone onboard; they had stripped our dead of their weapons, clothes, and gear. Our new plan was to hit the same target again but arrive by helicopter to avoid the IEDs, then snatch up our terrorist targets before they could get out of their beds.

April 5, 2007

A few nights after the IED incident, our intel trigger was pulled on the same target. While the choppers readied and our guys geared up in our team's ready room, Gary Blackwell and I rolled across Camp Fallujah to alert our Iraqi scouts to get ready. We never disclosed our target locations to the scouts; we just gave them a heads-up that we were rolling and to get jocked up. I always had to assume that there was an intel leak, even if there wasn't.

I would be the assault force commander on this mission. We were a mixed group, a combination of twenty-two opera-tors made up of Navy SEALs and our Iraqi scouts. This was a turnover operation, which meant our newly arrived SEAL teammates from Team 10 would be on the mission with us. For some of our newly arrived SEALs, this would be their first ever mission, and for others it would be their first operation of this deployment.

Meanwhile, Iraq's Sunni–Shia factional violence was out of control; American troops were pouring into Iraq to quell the fighting in a strategy referred to as "the Surge." Iran and other state actors were provoking and supporting the violence, and there was a mix of low- and high-level criminal activity, plus a steady stream of terrorists from across the globe coming into Iraq to fight. The violence was constant, and it was tearing the country apart, killing countless Iraqis as well as American ser-vice members.

Our mission on this particular night was to capture or kill an al-Qaida terrorist cell leader in a safe house under the cover of darkness, and by complete surprise. This cell leader knew how to move, hide, shoot, fight, and kill. He came with a loyal crew of fanatical bodyguards. Our enemy target in Fallujah had been shooting down medevac helicopters with our own ground-to-air missiles. These missiles, and other equipment, had been acquired by the enemy during an ambush of a U.S. Army convoy in Ramadi just west of our location. The helicopters that they shot down may have also given them access to our radios, weapons, and night-vision equipment. Being experts at target takedowns, none of that bothered us. We were so silent on missions, we could come up on our targets—terrorists, rapists, and murderers—still sound asleep in their beds, their weapons parked beside them.

We believed our terrorist target was holed up in a single-story, walled compound in northeast Fallujah. Iraqi compounds are a confusing jigsaw of small buildings with windowless rooms and multiple doors. The kit I wore on missions was always the same, except for this night. (A kit is what SEALs wear to work. It's like a tool belt, and it's customized to one's role on the team and previous experience in gunfights.) I dressed and set up my kit the same way I had done for hundreds of other missions: my Kevlar helmet with Night Optic Devices (NODs) attached, cammies (my usual dark camouflage-colored cargo pants and shirt), Load Bearing Equipment (LBE) webbing over the body armor to carry extra pistol magazines, my radio, a tourniquet. A utility belt with pouches to carry a medical blowout kit, flash crashes, grenades and explosives for breaching doors. On this night I moved my pistol magazines from my left hip to the pocket located at the center of my vest. This was the first, last, and only time that I have moved my magazines. I'm not sure what prompted me to do it.

My kit was heavy, close to eighty pounds. My primary weapon, an M4 rifle, hung down from a sling in my front, and a radio system was strapped to my chest. My extra magazines full of 5.56- and 9-millimeter bullets were now tucked in the vest webbing wrapped around the front of my abdomen. My secondary weapon, a 9-millimeter pistol, I had strapped securely to my right leg. Underneath it all, like a rhinoceros's armor, were my bulletproof plates, protecting me from both the front and the back, and I always wore black gloves.

It was after midnight when the helicopters dropped us off about three clicks from the target, making the hike longer than usual. It was a rural area, speckled with small farms and not many homes. It was chilly, in the low sixties, but I was dripping wet with sweat, humping nearly eighty pounds of gear through the darkness.

The route took us through a small vineyard with trellis vines reaching up to our shoulders. The vines had woken from their winter dormancy, and there was already a canopy of young leaves on the branches, their regrowth triggered by the warm April sun. It was strange to find a lone vineyard in the middle of the desert. We walked leaning forward, bending low and blending into the outstretched arms of the vines as we moved through the narrow rows.

My internal dialogue, the voice in my head, shuts off once the mission begins. There is only the here and now; nothing else matters. My body and mind unite, and I become like an antenna tuned into everything around me—smells, sounds, tastes, and the slightest change in my surroundings. I can feel everyone's energy and am constantly assessing their condition by their pace, breathing tempo, and whispered grunts or lack thereof. It feels more like I'm floating rather than walking, constantly absorbing information from my environment and making automatic micro adjustments to improve our situation.

Suddenly there was a splash. We all paused, weapons ready—my heart rate spiking hard enough I could feel it thumping under my chest plate. A few seconds later, one of my SEAL teammates emerged from an irrigation ditch; his moonlight swim left him drenched but it managed to lighten our collective mood. It could have been any one of us who fell into the ditch, which should have made us sympathetic, but it didn't, and his misstep was met with sarcastic comments. We had done hundreds of real-world missions and thousands more in training—as professional warfighters, we were hyper-focused but totally relaxed. This is all normal stuff, and the comments served as constant reminders of the hazards of war. The SEAL teams are different than other military units, there was no need for me or any of our leaders to reprimand our brother or tell him to be more careful; however, outside the SEAL teams, I have seen other commanders micromanage their warriors. We have come to understand that the relentless peer ribbings and dark humor were far more effective than lectures, and the ruthless ridicule served as friendly reminders of mistakes not to be made again. This is all a normal part of our continuous process of improvement.

April 6, 2007, 1:33 AM

We arrived on target undetected. Our breacher identified a possible location in the compound where we thought our guy might be held up. "Breacher" is an actual occupation on SEAL teams—there's even a breacher school. A breacher's sole mission is to reach the other side of any barrier, whether it's a door or a wall or a fence. His methods include mechanical, ballistic, explosive, and thermal breaching. Sometimes I would just turn a doorknob and walk into the room, or go around a thick wall and enter through an open gate. We once had a target we'd visited three different times over a period of several months—and sure enough on all three missions, the key was in the lock. All I had to do was turn the key, unlock the door, and walk in. I found it totally bizarre that the occupants of the home left a key in their locked door. But as long as you get to the other side, it's still considered a breach.

We were split into two groups, one covered the outside area, and the other moved inside to cover doors and clear rooms. Our breacher surveyed the entry door, then mechanically opened it. The door popped open, and a group of my SEAL teammates poured into the room. We had practiced this technique of room clearing for years. We moved without thinking. The room was empty—it was a prayer room, with only one way in and one way out. My radio broadcasted the information into my earpiece: "short room." This was the signal that the target was not there. Because there were no other doors inside this room that led to other parts of the home, the breach team needed to get out fast and breach another door. As one group exited the short room, I stood by the door to a foyer. I donkey-kicked the door to the foyer to open it, and my room-clearing train followed me in.

To get to the entrance of the foyer, we had to pass through an outdoor carport covered by a sheet metal roof. Clark Schwedler, who a few days before had been rocked by an IED blast driving to this same target, had been the first man into the prayer room. He ran out of that room, through the carport, and into the foyer, where he saw that I was holding security on two different doors. Clarkie quickly set up on the second door, located diagonally across from me. He was loaded down with extra weight, as he was hauling around all our intel-gathering gear. These were the types of compounds where we would often find gruesome video evidence of what the people who we hunted had done to women, to little boys and girls—while they made family members watch.

Our Iraqi scouts and SEALs followed Clarkie's lead and split off my room-clearing train to fill in behind him to create a second room-clearing train. Less than thirty seconds after entering the first room, Clarkie was at the front of another train ready to clear another room. Clark's door was located directly across from my door and the angle was such that a straight line could be drawn connecting the entryways of both doors. Through the open doors, you could see the far corner of one room from the far corner of the other room. It was pitch dark; however, the yellow glow of a gas lamp pilot in the corner of the foyer provided more than enough light to fuel my night-vision goggles. I could see everything clearly.

I was the number-one man on the door in my train, which meant I would be the first man into the room. Missions often included "debates" as to who would get to go first. All these guys were fearless and liked to "train hop" to the front of the stack—the most dangerous place—to be first into a room. SEALs love to fight. We all want to be the first into the fight, and every SEAL is willing to accept the greater risk, especially for his buddy's sake.

I had no apprehension about the possibility of my own death. My concern was for my platoonmates. While I can't speak for everyone, their actions this night proved they all felt the same way.

Clarkie and I looked at each other; he smiled back at me. We had practiced this maneuver a thousand times and had successfully done it on hundreds of missions just like this one. There was no rush of adrenaline or anxiety—we were composed, relaxed, and professional. We would simultaneously breach our respective doors and go to work clearing the rooms of enemy fighters and other potential threats. We launched on the signal: a mutual wave of our rifle barrels. I breached the door to my room; it swung open to the right. I followed the door in as it opened, looked down the right wall, and saw that it was clear.

As I pivoted off my right foot to move down the left wall, I had the sensation that my body was being slammed with a dozen sledgehammers. My entire body was now in the room, and the men behind me in my room-clearing train were attempting to follow me in. The room was small, twelve feet by twelve feet; my night-vision goggles illuminated the darkness, and I saw in clear view four of our targets aiming at me. All of them armed with automatic weapons and *all of them firing* at me.

It was surreal, like something out of a movie: time slowed almost to a stop and everything happened in super slow motion, almost as if I were watching the scene unfold frame by frame. Seconds seemed like minutes. A slow-motion torrent of bullets flew at me. I could clearly see all the bullets coming at me. I had total auditory exclusion; there were no sounds. I had never been shot before, so I had no idea how it felt. In this strange slow-motion scene, I had a mental conversation with myself: *Hey, am I actually getting shot right now?* It occurred to me that those sledgehammers smashing all over my body were bullets hitting me, one after another after another.

It was in that moment I said my first real prayer: "God, please get me home to my girls." My wife and two young daughters were halfway around the world; in that instant, I felt them and they felt me.

It felt like I was a bullet-dodging character in *The Matrix*, only I wasn't dodging any of the bullets; they were hitting me. My rifle was shot out of my hands. Bullets whizzing past my head hammered into the men entering the room behind me even as I continued to penetrate down the left wall. Nobody else in my train would be able to make entry, as all four of the enemy continued to fire directly into what is known as the fatal funnel, the dimly lit doorway in which I was standing.

War shifts from a national interest to an extremely personal one. This shift happens at the precise moment enemy bullets are directed at you and not at a theology or a country. It's also at this precise moment when self-preservation becomes the overriding objective. When bullets start flying and men are dying, nobody is thinking about "God and country"; our thoughts are about our loved ones at home, the guys beside us, and ending the fight. I suspect that during these violent episodes, the enemy thinks and reacts much the same way. In the violence we become more human, more ruthless, and more alike than we are different. Survival is all that matters. In the savagery, our involuntary responses are powered by our respective autonomic nervous systems. This internal fight-or-flight ecosystem has been installed in the most ancient part of every brain over the course of human evolution and our reactions are governed by primal survival instincts.

The enemy bullets triggered my rage and drove me to act; it was then that my body became my mind and took over. I suppose that's what a habit is, when the body overrides the mind and acts without specific instructions from the brain. My right hand instinctively reached down for my secondary weapon, a pistol. My hand was on autopilot as it unhooked the rubber strap I had fashioned to keep my pistol secure, and with a fluid forward push and pull—the very same motion that I had done a hundred thousand times in training—my weapon released from my holster.

I aimed my pistol and engaged the enemy fighter directly opposite me down the left wall. He was glaring at me, with his weapon throwing rounds directly at me. I returned fire; four or five rounds from my weapon caught him in the face and chest as he stared at me. His head jilted back; I saw the life leave his eyes like a light going off. I knew he was dead as he melted into a pile in front of me. I landed next to the dead man on my left side. Years of training and muscle memory without any direct orders from my brain lifted my arm, arched it, and aimed my pistol at a young male figure—maybe in his early twenties—as he stood up and moved toward the doorway. I was still on the floor when I watched him pull a hand grenade from the front of his vest and pull the pin. My right hand pointed at him, and my index finger squeezed the trigger. I saw the bullets exit my pistol and spin clockwise as they flew toward him, leaving a green vapor trail in their wake. I watched my bullets punch into one side of his head, an exhaust of blood and brain matter instantly exiting out the other side. I shot him dead as he attempted a suicide mission to run out into the foyer with a live grenade where my fellow SEALs and Iraqi scouts had stacked up, attempting to enter the room. My rounds dropped him in his tracks; as he fell forward, I saw the grenade release from his hand and roll toward me. Then it detonated.

One of our newly arrived SEALs from Team 10 was outside under the carport looking into the room's only window when he saw my bullets hit the enemy in the head. He watched as the enemy fell. The ensuing grenade blast shattered the window, spraying shards of glass into my teammate's face. This was his first mission in Iraq—what a way to start a new job.

The grenade blast knocked me unconscious. When I awoke a few minutes later, I was fully lucid and lying on my left side, looking across the room at two men; both were firing their weapons over my head out the window directly above me. The grenade blast had twisted my helmet, rendering my night-vision goggles unusable. The light from their muzzle flashes and the dim glow of the gas lamp in the foyer were enough to clearly illuminate the men standing no more than ten feet away from me.

I heard no sounds; it was totally silent. I was in a very bad place in the middle of a gunfight—if the enemy caught a glimpse of me glaring up at them, all it would take to finish me off would be for both of them to point down, pull their triggers, and unload high-velocity bullets into me. If I could clearly see them, then they could see me too. For an instant, I thought about playing dead, but in that same millisecond, before the thought could be fully evaluated, my anger rejected it outright. I had never been so angry—a feeling of determined, ruthless rage. It seemed to be stored somewhere deep inside me, and something just snapped. In that moment, my rage consumed me; my world closed in and nothing else mattered to me but destroying the two men still standing in front of me. I would fight back and kill them before they killed me.

I didn't know it at the time, but while I was lying unconscious on the floor, two of my SEAL teammates were still outside the door of the room trying to get a shot at the enemy. Two of our Iraqi counterparts were the only eyes that saw me enter that room; in the chaos that ensued, they were unable to communicate my location to anyone. The volume of fire coming from the room through the door and out of the window was so excessive that there was no way anyone else was getting into the room. The team decided to pull everyone back and call in an air strike to "neutralize" the target—and me with it.

As the team pulled back from the house, Connor, my other SEAL teammate, was shot and wounded by one of the two remaining enemy fighters firing over my head out the window. While I lay on the floor, my teammates worked their radios, calling for the status of each other and what was going on in the house. I heard nothing.

As the remaining elements of my assault team departed the house and moved to a safe dropping distance from the target, I was lying on my left side with my pistol still in my right hand. Just like before, my arm reached up and aimed at one of the men standing in front of me and my finger pulled the trigger. I couldn't hear the gun fire, but I felt my hand jump—rounds exited my weapon and I watched the projectiles fly in slow motion as they punched into his body. Small holes burst open in the fabric of his shirt where my bullets entered. His face contorted into a bizarre combination of surprise and pain—more surprise than pain. In less than five seconds, I ran a magazine dry and completed a magazine change before the two enemy fighters figured out that I was still alive and shooting back at them. My bullets drew their gunfire away from my departing teammates. Their full attention and bullets were then directed back at me.

I still don't have an explanation as to why I moved my magazines from my left hip to the webbing in the front of my vest, but it saved my life, and possibly the lives of many others that night. I was lying on my left side, which is where I normally carried my extra magazines—on my left hip. They would have been trapped under me if they had been in their usual location.

The enemy fighters were now both so close to me. I remember the stunned look on their faces as they pointed their weapons at me and I fired back. A round from one of their AK-47s struck the bottom of my pistol and dislodged my gun's magazine. My pistol jammed, and I felt the gun's grips crumble in my hand. Another enemy bullet sailed clear through the foot of my magazine. I opened my hand slightly to release the shards of broken plastic that were once my pistol grips—the grips seemed to absorb the shock, shattering like an armor plate. I was fortunate to have this type of weapon; another model may have been smashed to bits or been shot out of my hands.

My palm was now pressed against the gun's internal springs. The bullets that struck my pistol caused my weapon to malfunction; I squeezed the trigger, but nothing happened. I quickly cleared the malfunction with a tap of the bottom of the magazine to firmly reinsert it into the pistol, a rack of the slide, then I squeezed the trigger. I had done this "tap, rack, bang" malfunction drill so many times that it happened automatically. All the while, I was still being shot at from no more than ten feet away. An instant later, well before the human brain could process *what* and *how* it had happened, my hand aimed my pistol at the other man standing across from me, and my finger squeezed the trigger. I saw rounds twisting as they exited my pistol, flying toward him and entering his body, and then a round tunneled into his face. Science has termed this slow-motion phenomenon as *time's subjective expansion.*

I emptied that magazine into both men as they crumpled to the floor in front of me. I loaded my last magazine into my damaged pistol. I was lying on my left side, leaning against the man who I first shot when I entered the room. I pushed myself up with one hand and reached behind with the other, placing my pistol against my dead enemy's motionless body and fired several more rounds.

Seconds later, all four enemy fighters were silent; their dead bodies lay in pools of their own blood and piles of spent bullet casings. A metallic odor flooded the room. Blood and urine leaked from their bodies onto the floor.

I knew that I had been shot. I felt heavy, like there was a few hundred pounds sitting on my back; it was difficult to breathe. The fight was not over, and the worst battles were yet to come.

CHAPTER 3

Resiliency Training

A curse on him who begins life in gentleness.

—Pastor André Trocmé, Hero of the
French Resistance in WWII

He looked huge, like a damn monster. She was screaming and fighting back, which only made it worse. I was frozen in terror. He bent her arm over his knee and like a twig cracked it. I watched him break her arm. He yelled at me, "Go get me a glass of water." I ran to the kitchen, filled a glass, and ran back to hand it to him; he drank it, then smashed the glass on a nearby table and held the broken shard like a knife. He went after her again with his newly created blade. I jumped on his back to stop him. I think that's what finally snapped him out of his uncontrolled rage. I flew off him as he swung his arm and I landed on the ground on my back. He spun to attack his unknown aggressor and realized it was me. I clearly remember seeing his expression dissolve from rage into one of guilt and shame.

This is my earliest memory, and my first encounter with a terrorist. It was 1976 in New Jersey—and the terrorist was my father. His victim was my mother. I was five years old.

Fact is that violence and abuse is a learned behavior. My father acquired it from his father. He was a victim who became a perpetrator. My father never really talked about his childhood, but I'm sure it was rough. The stories I learned of his upbringing came via third parties, family members who would occasionally discuss my grandfather's violence, how he destroyed his family over time. There were stories of extreme mental, emotional, and physical trauma. My grandfather, who I never met, was either out of control or acting out his own transferred childhood traumas. I have to believe that no person in their right mind would subject their spouse and children to such extreme behavior as chasing them around with a butcher knife. My father was one of three siblings, all of whom experienced life-altering childhood trauma at the hands of their parents, trauma that carried over into the rest of their lives. My aunt was so mentally shattered early in her childhood by her father that she entered an inpatient psychiatric facility at age ten and remained there until she passed. I wonder what my grandparents' mother and father were... to make the monsters they made.

My parents divorced not long after my father broke my mother's arm. My mother would soon start dating and would eventually marry Tom, a black man, a rare union in the 1970s. My father held racist beliefs and my mother's marriage to a black man inflamed my father's racist sentiment. The divorce included a custody hearing. I was young, but I can distinctly recall someone in court—a lawyer, possibly the judge—asking me strange questions about Tom, like *Have you ever seen Tom naked?* and *Have you ever seen Tom and your mother sleeping together?* The focus of the custody battle, which should have been on my father and his treatment of us, was instead trained on me, an innocent bystander.

Interracial relationships were not the social norm in the

1970s. I'm sure the court knew my father beat my mother and us kids, but they still awarded him full custody regardless. My hunch is that the courts were so biased at that time, they decided my younger brother and I would be better off with a wife beater and an abusive father than be raised by an interracial couple.

My mother was young herself, still in her early twenties. She did her best to save my brother and me, but she barely had the power to save herself. I don't blame her for wanting to escape a life of terror, one in which she was regularly beaten. My mother lost the custody battle, and my brother and I were to live with my father. She must have been devastated.

My father was a sailor. When the Navy issued him new orders, we moved to Pennsylvania from New Jersey. After the divorce, my father remarried. Our new stepmother soon became pregnant, first giving birth to my half sister. Two years later, she gave birth to my half brother. Trauma attracts trauma—it has its own distinct language and behaviors. We would be raised by two people who had been severely traumatized as children.

My new stepmother was a natural fit for our family. She, too, had a history of childhood abuse, both physical and mental. I don't know much about the early years of her life, other than her parents would lock her in a closet for long periods of time. She was put up for adoption and taken in by a loving couple. My stepmother would grow up to be both victim and perpetrator. She would alternate between coercing my father to beat us and slapping us around herself. She and my father would get into their own fights too—she would fight back, even though she had no way of winning, as he was six foot two and weighed 240 pounds. He would bring me to the basement where he kept his weights and have me spot him, even though I was nowhere near strong enough to help. He was old man strong and would stack four 45-pound plates on each side of a 45-pound bar and press the 405 pounds off his chest.

One of the worst beatings I ever endured came when I was eight. My brother and I had gone out one winter day and pelted a car with snowballs. The driver was pissed, but if he'd known the price we were about to pay for our transgression, he may have given us a pass. We ran to our house with the driver of the car chasing us. He knocked on our front door and told my parents what we had done. My father and stepmother had a friend over at the time and they were all drinking. My parents were outraged. Our father sent us to the basement, an ad hoc torture chamber of sorts, where he made us strip naked before tying our hands to a pole, so we were facing each other. He whipped us with his belt so hard that after fifteen minutes, he'd worked up a sweat; all the while, my stepmother and her friend sat on the basement steps sipping their booze, urging him to beat us harder, and longer. When he was done, my brother and I were both badly bloodied and bruised.

My father's violence escalated as we grew. He would smear toothpaste on the nylon belt when he whipped us so it would sting as it cut and bruised us. I'm not sure where he picked up this technique, but it worked. His routine was to bring me into the basement and make me drop my pants, so that my bare ass was available. He would wind up and rip into my bare backside with that belt, holding on to my arm as I twisted in a circle, trying to escape. I recall a week that was prefaced with him telling us, "I know that you will be bad kids this week." He beat us bloody, and then he went to work. This was some crazy stuff; he was so nuts that he set his alarm for 4:00 a.m. to wake us all up to beat us for no reason whatsoever before he went to work. We got beat and went back to bed—hardly a typical morning routine for a first grader.

My early childhood was a real-life horror movie I couldn't escape. One Halloween he waited until it was dark and cut the power to all the lights in the house. He put on a Halloween album that played haunted house sound effects, turned up the volume, put on a terrifying mask, and proceeded to chase us through the house, growling and yelling at the top of his lungs. It scared the crap out of me to the point where I ended up having vivid nightmares because of it, a recurring nightmare in which I was being stalked by a monster; this dream haunted me for years. In it, I would make it to my room just in time to grab the doorknob, twist it, and push the door open. As it swung forward, my legs would fly up and my belly would just make it over the top of the door when the monster grabbed my feet and tried to pull me away screaming. Nightmares, like all dreams, enter the subconscious mind through conscious experiences.

One time my father piled us all in the car to take us to the circus. We were so excited. We had been driving for about five minutes when he said, "Why am I taking you miserable kids to the circus?" He then slapped me, turned the car around, and drove home. We never went to the circus.

Growing up was a strange combination of violence, structure, chaos, and uncertainty, but that combination was such an ingrained part of our lives, it became routine. We did our homework every evening before dinner, which was always at six o'clock. We had a set bedtime. Every Saturday my younger brother and I had to scrub all the bathrooms in our house, and every Sunday my stepmother would make pancakes and waffles. If anyone disrupted the routine, the consequences were severe.

Over time, my brother and I found more and more ways to stay out of the house. In the fall, after we raked the leaves in our yard, we would earn money by raking the neighbors' yards.

We did the same in the winter, shoveling snow from around our house, then make decent cash digging out the neighbors' driveways. We would spend countless hours at our local golf course, searching the ponds and roughs for lost golf balls. We would sell the balls back to the golfers and then ride our bikes to the roller rink to blow all our hard-earned money.

I played soccer and our team won every game. I was a pitcher on my Little League team, but we lost every game. I could throw hard, but I had no control. I once chucked a pitch over the backstop, and I hit so many batters that the umpire thought I was hitting kids intentionally. My pitching style was sort of a metaphor for my life: hard, fast, and out of control. My family was dysfunctional, albeit I didn't understand it as dysfunction—it was my normal. My father would beat my ass and then sit with me for hours drilling me on multiplication flash cards until I knew them cold. I simply thought everyone's parents beat the snot out of their kids and drank until they passed out.

I did eventually learn that my family was not like everyone else's. One day, my father made me and my brother each wear a T-shirt to our swim team practice to cover the welts and bruises on our backs. I guess when you're a kid you have few reference points to compare family function or lack thereof. I remember seeing the red and blue welts on my little brother's back through his wet T-shirt. Somehow, I knew that we needed to hide our wounds, that the welts my father's beating caused were bad and wrong. I didn't understand the complexity of emotions formed in that moment. This is how trauma distorts: the beatings were wrong, having to hide the evidence of my father's violence was wrong, our family's dysfunction was wrong, me and my brother were made to feel wrong, but we were just little kids.

I credit my father for training me to overcome fear at a very young age, or at least to manage it. One of his unintended methods was to make me go diving in a local creek and look for wallets and other items that drunken partiers lost when they went swimming in their cutoff jeans with valuables in their pockets. After the first few dives, I eventually learned to stop fearing the dark, but I remember the cold, black water to this day.

Finally, at the age of twelve, after years of enduring his drunken rages and endless beatings, I decided to fight back. One night, I found him passed out drunk on the couch. I knew that he was passed out because the crotch of his blue jeans was darkened from having wet himself. I grabbed a baseball bat and walked back and forth for about five minutes, debating my intended actions until I finally mustered up my courage, and with an overhead ax swing, I drilled him hard on the chest with the baseball bat. It felt great, a totally empowering rush. I didn't kill him but I sure surprised him, because he immediately woke up from his booze-induced blackout with a look of total confusion that quickly turned evil. He looked at the bat in my hands and realized that was what had just bounced off his chest. I knew by the look in his eyes that he was going to kill me. He chased me upstairs to my room, where I jumped out of my second-story window into a thorny rosebush. I looked up to see my enraged father stick his head out only to pull it back in. I could hear his pounding footsteps from outside as he ran downstairs. He was determined to hunt me down, chasing me through the woods around our house in the dark. He couldn't get through the thick underbrush, but I was too terrified to slow down. He never caught me. I spent the night at a neighbor's house, and by the next day when I returned home, he'd forgotten all about the incident.

In 1983, my father was transferred to Miramar, near San

Diego, California. That's where he totally lost it. He was drinking, causing problems at work, and had been arrested several times for defecating in the aisles of stores. Some mental health professionals describe this peculiar public display as "elimination disorder." It's a behavior that has been identified in several serial killers and manifests out of extreme anger at someone or something.

I was twelve years old when my stepmother received word that my father would be medically discharged from the Navy and institutionalized with schizophrenia and a host of other psychiatric conditions. He would spend the rest of his life in an inpatient facility or in an assisted living environment. My father has since died; he was very sick and really broken. He did a terrible job as a parent; however, I know now that he did the best he could. I don't hold any harsh feelings toward him.

I was about twelve or thirteen years old when my stepmother became our legal guardian and seized her newfound freedom by dating a guy in a local rock 'n' roll band named Beachy and hosting parties at our house. Our home quickly turned into a constant party, with its own in-house band and all the characters that came with it. People—strangers—would sit around my house all day getting drunk and stoned. I would catch my stepmother and Beachy having sex, which they never tried to hide. On one particular occasion, my stepmother was partying with Beachy and his band of losers when she tried to smack me. I caught her arm, spun it behind her back, then swept her legs out from under her, dumping her on her ass. That episode got me and my brother sent to Maine to live with our maternal grandparents—who we hadn't seen in years—for the summer. My half siblings were still young at the time. I still remember looking over my shoulder and seeing my half brother lying in his crib and my half sister in her bed as I made my way out of the house.

The move to Maine would mark the last time we would ever live with our stepmother. That fall, my brother and I moved from Maine to Virginia Beach to live with our mother and her second husband, Tom. It was only after we arrived that I learned about how my stepmother and my father had deliberately and systematically tried to alienate me and my brother from our mother. She showed us a box filled with years' worth of birthday and Christmas cards that had been returned without the checks she'd written for us. My father and stepmother had cashed them all and kept the money for themselves. Despite this, I feel the same about my stepmother as I do my father— she survived my father's violence and did the best she could. I don't hold any harsh feelings toward her, either.

Tom and my mother never hit us; they were patient and did their best to parent some severely abused young minds. If the courts had not been so biased, we could have skipped the seven years of abuse and lived in Virginia Beach all along. But, as I would come to learn, everything happens for a reason.

We arrived in Virginia Beach right as I was about to start the eighth grade and my brother into grade six. As the new kids in school, my brother and I were easy targets and we got picked on. I never started any fights, but never backed away from them either. I made it through the eighth grade and entered Green Run High School, where I lasted until my junior year, when my wrestling coach caught me smoking pot in a school bathroom. This caused my expulsion. Shortly after being expelled, I had a run-in with the police. A cop busted me with a bag of weed. At the time, any amount over an ounce was a felony. The cop grabbed the bag and asked, "Is this an ounce?"

I said, "Yes."

He opened the bag, grabbed a pinch, and chucked it onto the street, then said: "Is it an ounce now?"

"No," I replied.

That cop saved me from a felony charge and may have even saved my life. I'd like to find that guy one day and thank him.

After being expelled from high school, I ended up at Job Corps, a vocational residential training program for troubled teens and young adults up to age twenty-one. There were kids from all over the country, mostly from the big cities, including those in Baltimore, Kentucky, and New York. There was an older kid who would pick on me, but only when he was surrounded by his friends. The shop teacher told us both to go out back and sort it out, but the guy wouldn't go anywhere without his entourage. One afternoon, I was up on a ladder doing carpentry on the second story of a barn when the same kid kicked the ladder out from under me. I dropped ten feet to the ground and grabbed a two-by-four stud on the rebound. I bounced up, and in one swift motion, I drilled him over the head with it. His eyes rolled back in his skull and he passed out. An ambulance had to be called to take him away.

Crowning a kid with a two-by-four secured my reputation as the "crazy white dude who would clock you over the dome with something if you messed with him." That reputation was helpful, as the Job Corps student body was a little rough. I earned my GED and graduated the program with a journeyman's carpentry license, then started a construction job. Neither the GED nor the job stopped me from getting into trouble. I was always getting caught drinking, smoking pot, and fighting.

It was about this time in 1988 when a neighbor—a retired Navy diver—offered a suggestion: "You are going to end up dead or in jail if you keep this up. You should join the SEAL teams instead—they'll pay you to do all the things you're getting in trouble doing now." He may not have known it then, but his assessment of me was extremely accurate. I sort of took his suggestion and visited a local Armed Services recruiting office with the intention of joining the Marines. It was 1988 and the Marines rejected me because of my GED.

Turns out, 1988 was an anomaly for the USMC: that year, the Marines only accepted candidates with high school diplomas. No offense to my Marine brothers, but these are the guys who jokingly refer to themselves as "crayon eaters," and they wouldn't accept *me*? Fortunately, the Marine recruiter I met with sent me down the hall to the Navy recruiter, who was more than willing to take me.

As a child, I didn't know that trauma and resiliency would become my default programming, or how much it would shape my thoughts, beliefs, relationships, and behaviors. Fortunately, my childhood trauma made me a good fit for military service— a study has since found that military service members and veterans were twice as likely as nonmembers to have experienced childhood trauma; or, as the study calls it, adverse childhood experiences (ACEs).* This same statistic is also true for most prison inmates.

That conversation I had back in 1988 with my Navy diver neighbor was prophetic. In some ways, it feels like the universe conspired to place me in the Navy. After all, so many things needed to line up perfectly for me to become a sailor: the cop who saved me from a felony arrest, for starters, which would

---

* JR Blosnich, et al. "Disparities in Adverse Childhood Experiences (ACE) Among Individuals with a History of Military Service," *JAMA Psychiatry* 71, no. 9 (2014): 1041–48.

have prevented me from military service altogether. My rejection from the Marine Corps was fortunate too—I never would have had a long career in the Marines. They're way too structured for me.

I was fortunate. Many who experience childhood trauma like my own end up in prison, or worse. The SEAL teams would offer me an amazing home, and a second family. It would be a place for me to channel my anger and aggression, practice self-discipline, build my self-esteem, and hone my leadership skills. In that recruiting office, the Navy offered me the chance to travel the globe and have amazing adventures with the greatest group of people on the planet.

My childhood was not exactly idyllic, but it's what happened to me and I'm very grateful for all of it. The wounds of my childhood trauma served as the foundation of some truly excellent resiliency training. Resiliency is a conditioned response to physical and emotional trauma and stress. It's been a never-ending process of understanding, endurance, evaluation, acceptance, and application that continues to help me get through some very difficult situations. Childhood trauma, especially the kind perpetrated by parents, can be some of the most damaging because it can cause children to feel unlovable. Some children who feel unlovable can become unlovable adults, and some of those become unlovable parents, thus repeating the cycle. The unlovable live lonely, tragic lives. If my hurts, mistakes, butt-whippings, and insights can help you overcome yours, then this book has value for both of us.

CHAPTER 4

Boot Camp to BUD/S

I entered the Navy's delayed entry program. The Navy recruiter guaranteed that I would have an opportunity to attend BUD/S training. BUD/S is SEAL school, the place where guys train and qualify to become Navy SEALs. The SEALs operate on sea, air, and land. That means everywhere. We've even had several SEALs become astronauts. (Part of me thinks we should capitalize that last *s* in SEALs for *Space*.) The occupation is everything Hollywood and the media have made it out to be: dangerous, exciting, and filled with adventure.

After signing on the dotted line, I spent the next six months working out and doing my best not to get into trouble until I finally boarded a bus for the trip to the Military Entry Processing Station (MEPS) facility in southern Virginia. MEPS is the weigh station for all new military recruits. There, I found myself part of an interesting blend of Americana, one that included all shapes, sizes, colors, and temperaments of young men and women who were leaving the civilian world and getting their first taste of the United States military.

Once processed, I boarded another bus at MEPS and proceeded to sit through a fourteen-hour ride to Illinois to begin my career in the Navy. I arrived at Great Lakes, the home of the Navy's boot camp, on January 4, 1989. The instructors quickly moved us all inside out of the cold. Within the first hour, I was issued a new hairstyle, stripped to my undershorts, and told to find my place in a long line of recruits. I held my newly issued Navy uniform—complete with dog bowl hat—in front of me as I passed through the inoculation station where a guy with a gun injected something into my right arm, while another guy simultaneously shot a few different vaccines into my left.

I never in my life wanted to quit anything more than I did Navy boot camp. For me, boot camp was mind-numbing. I can endure almost anything but boredom. People think that I'm strange when I say that for me boot camp was way more challenging than BUD/S. There was only one time, on the very last day of BUD/S Hell Week, that I thought to myself, *What am I doing here?* Ten minutes later, we were secured and Hell Week was over. But the entire time I was at boot camp, I kept thinking, *What the hell am I doing here?* I didn't have many other options, though, and quitting was the least attractive of them all. To me, quitting a hard task is a form of cheating. If I'd quit boot camp, I would only have been cheating myself of all the benefits and resiliency gained from enduring the suffer-fest. I have found it's better to hunker down, remain calm, and keep going.

The January weather meant it was too cold to send us outside to train, so we did indoor workouts, which were not very challenging. Company commanders would yell, "Let's make it rain in here!" and a few hundred of us recruits would do push-ups and shove our metal bunkbed "racks" around until our collective body heat made condensation build up and drip from the windows. I was still bored stiff, so I attempted to volunteer for the morning physical training (PT) session—at 4:00 a.m. I needed to train for the SEAL qualification test, and boot camp was making me fat and slow. The 4:00 a.m. PT sessions were reserved as punishment for infractions made by recruits. I guess it worked because they punished me by not allowing me to participate.

I was seventeen years old and had way too much pent-up energy. Since I couldn't sleep at night, I worked out in the bathroom. I think the company commanders saw some potential in me, and they knew that I was bored because I kept volunteering to wake up at 4:00 a.m. to do what most people dreaded. They decided to give me some extra responsibility and made me my division's recruit master-at-arms. I was placed in a division with sixteen other guys who were determined to win every boot camp competition flag—a system intended to promote team-work. I needed the competition to keep me focused on something other than the monotony of marching, making my rack, and cleaning. Our division ended up winning every competition flag.

In February of 1989, near the end of boot camp, I was administered the SEAL screening test. There were about fifty of us taking tests for different Navy specialties like diver, SEAL, and EOD (Explosive Ordinance Disposal) technician. I was one of three who passed the SEAL qualification test. Out of the fifty candidates, less than twenty qualified for any program.

There was only about a week remaining before graduation when I got into a scuffle. One guy kept messing with me, and on this particular night, I'd caught him sticking his boogers on my pillow. An argument broke out, and then—almost like it was planned—the company commander opened the door just in time to see me take a swing at the guy. The door happened to be directly behind my rack, so the commander had a front-row seat to what would be my first and last fight in boot camp.

As punishment, I was rolled back into another class and not allowed to graduate with the group I'd been training with for two months. I was frustrated and devastated. That night, I lay in my bed and cried. I did, however, attend my new class graduation ceremony in my new assignment as boot camp graduation parking lot attendant. Nobody was coming to see me graduate anyway. I'm not into pomp and circumstance and all the "pass and review" marching. I much preferred watching to participating, so my punishment turned out to be well worth it. Everything always works out for me, just not the way I expect it to. I have come to learn that exercising patience permits for an alternate and sometimes equally (if not preferred) outcome.

After I was rolled back, I experienced the hardest job in my twenty-one years in the Navy: KP, or kitchen patrol. I gained a whole new respect for our Navy cooks and kitchen crew. It was a ton of hard, messy, time-consuming work: I prepped huge quantities of food and then, after everyone ate, I would scrub massive pots until they were sparkling clean and it was time for the next meal. Then I would go back to prep. That's all I did for a whole week: prepping and scrubbing. After dinner, the entire KP crew would sweep and mop the chow hall floor, which was the signal for the rats to come out. One rat in particular was a cat-sized monster we named Ralph. We would all chase after Ralph, screaming and swinging our brooms at him, but we never got him. I'm glad, honestly—I think Ralph's presence and our reaction to him released our pent-up stress, and we looked forward to seeing him every night. KP was hard work, but a necessary part of my real-world education. It humbled me, and it was so exhausting, I slept like a baby every night that week.

Eventually, I managed to graduate from boot camp. I believe Navy boot camp gives everyone the lessons they need when they need them. It's designed a lot like life itself: it identifies our individual flaws, highlights our weaknesses, and forces us to adapt accordingly. If we have the humility and will to recognize them, we can train to correct our flaws and eliminate our weaknesses. I was impatient and had to learn to deal with it. When I was weak, I had to learn to be strong. When I was fearful, I had to learn courage. When I felt terror, I had to learn to find calm and focus. All the lessons built the confidence required to get through the next test. We are all a combination of blessings and curses—for some people the curses might be a physical weakness, while others may have confidence issues. I gained the much-needed ability to overcome boredom, frailty, and fear, or at least find a way to endure them.

In today's Navy, recruits who complete boot camp and have a contract for BUD/S go directly to Coronado, California, to begin their SEAL qualification process. I didn't have that opportunity. After my extended stay at boot camp, I checked into A-School, which was conveniently located on the same frozen facility as boot camp. A-School is designed to train a person with zero mechanical experience, like me, to become a competent machinist in about sixty days. I have to hand it to the Navy: A-School training delivered results exactly as advertised. I scored the third highest on the final exam, earning my Machinist Mate rating. Shortly thereafter, I received new orders to attend Nuclear Machinist Mate C-School for additional training, and then join the crew aboard the nuclear-powered aircraft carrier, the USS *Carl Vinson*.

C-School? Aircraft carrier? I almost lost my mind. The recruiter had guaranteed me a slot at BUD/S; I'd passed the physical qualification test, I had done everything the Navy asked me to do, and now they were going back on their promise to send me to BUD/S. I stomped across the facility to the base commander's office, where I told his secretary I needed a meeting.

"I need to see the commander." He was a Navy captain; I was a seventeen-year-old E-2 (I had been an E-3, but the Navy busted me down a rank after the altercation). The captain was probably curious what was on my mind, so he had me come in for a talk. I explained that the Navy had screwed up my orders and that I should be going to BUD/S. He wrote down some notes and explained the chain of command to me and said he would investigate it. I knew full well that I was going to be punished for skipping over my chain of command and going directly to the base commander, but I didn't care. What's the worst that they could do to me? Navy boot camp and the various punishments I'd endured there didn't even come close to my father's brand of punishment. He had trained me to tolerate all manner of physical and psychological pain.

BUD/S

I had just turned eighteen when I flew from Great Lakes, Illinois, to the Navy facility in Coronado, California, to attend Basic Underwater Demolition/SEAL school. At the time, BUD/S training was divided into four phases, the first of which was Basic Conditioning and was titled "Fourth Phase." It's not really training—more like four weeks of physical challenges and cold-water immersion. First Phase culminates with Hell Week, which begins at sundown on Sunday and ends on Friday.

(Second and Third Phases have since traded places in the SEAL training sequence.) Second Phase is now the Combat Dive Phase. My BUD/S Second Phase was land warfare training, which consisted of more PT, basic weapons handling, blowing things up, and land navigation training. Most of this training was done on San Clemente Island, off the coast of Southern California. Third Phase was combat dive training, which—in my opinion—was the most challenging.

Fourth Phase: The Holding Pen

Fourth Phase included a mix of guys: new recruits like me who had yet to be assigned to a BUD/S class and others who had been rolled back from previous classes for injuries or other issues. My first time through Fourth Phase lasted about two weeks and consisted primarily of physical conditioning, mostly calisthenics, running, swimming, and obstacle course or O-course reps.

On my second day of Fourth Phase, we did a timed four-mile beach run in soft sand wearing boots and our old Underwater Demolition Team shorts—a holdover from the days before SEAL teams existed.

Soon, we were doing these runs on a weekly basis, and the stakes went up: if you didn't finish in time, you could be kicked out of BUD/S. Underwater Demolition Teams (UDTs) were the predecessors to the SEAL teams. Navy-issued UDT shorts were so short that when guys ran, their manhood would often sneak out the bottom. Plus, group beach runs were so fast-paced, guys had no time to stop and readjust their "man tackle." Apparently, a civilian group of female beachgoers who regularly spent time on the beach complained to the command about the unwelcome exposure, and running in UDT shorts was eventually banned. After that, we ran in long pants. I remember thinking I was in pretty good shape before the weekly runs, even though I was smoking about a half pack of cigarettes a day at that point. That soon changed—those timed runs smoked me, and I quit cigarettes.

Fourth Phase also included "new guy head shaving." There were several new guys who, after a few days into Fourth Phase, decided they wanted to take different career paths. Unfortunately, they were not allowed to quit just yet—first, they needed to be assigned to a BUD/S class. These "career changers" would then have their heads shaved, be assigned to a BUD/S class, and then be offered an opportunity to ring the bell and place their First Phase helmet on the quarter deck to signal that they were quitting the program. They would have to continue their careers in the Navy's floating fleet.

I began my BUD/S experience in Class 166 but wound up getting rolled back into class 168 due to a severe case of shin splints after Hell Week. I was rolled back again due to a personality difference with an instructor and ended up one of twenty-two graduates of BUD/S class 169, a class that had started out with about a hundred twenty guys.

Fourth Phase is also where I met my future wife. As a recruit, I was part of the forced labor crew for a Navy SEAL reunion event. In SEAL parlance, "forced labor" is otherwise referred to as being "voluntold." (The work options were far better if we volunteered, rather than waiting to be told to do something.)

The reunion was held on Coronado Beach, behind the SEAL facility. I was on the beach wearing my UDT shorts and white T-shirt, tending to the beer. Brenda was the guest of an older

SEAL and his wife. She had moved from North Carolina to San Diego and was working at a leather company and as a banquet server at the Hotel del Coronado. She asked if I was single, and we talked for hours after the event, right there on the beach. We dated exclusively from that day forward and married nine months later on Sunday, August 12, 1990. We spent our wedding night at the Hotel del Coronado, and I woke up Monday morning and ran down the beach to work. It was my last week of BUD/S; I was nineteen years old. As a child, I had been accustomed and attuned to harsh treatment. Brenda was the first person in my life to care for and nurture me. She made meals just for me and put notes of encouragement in my lunch box, she bandaged my wounds, and literally saved my life on more than one occasion.

First Phase: Physical Conditioning

If you are willing to work hard, be comfortable while being uncomfortable, be humble, and remain calm under stress, then you have a slim chance of making it through BUD/S. The average attrition rate is over 75 percent, and there was one class, BUD/S class 78, where everyone either failed or quit.

The first three weeks of BUD/S is an introduction to being extremely uncomfortable all the time, and about half of my class quit within that period, most of them ringing the bell after attempting one of three events—or evolutions, as they are known in BUD/S. The first evolution was the fifty-meter underwater swim. Basically, if you couldn't hold your breath and swim underwater for a full fifty meters, you were gone. "Drown Proofing" was the next eliminator. We were dumped into a fifteen-foot-deep Olympic-size pool with our hands tied behind our backs and our feet shackled together. The instructions were basically: "Don't drown." The actual test consisted of bobbing up and down from the bottom of the fifteen-foot deep end for fifteen minutes, float for ten minutes, pick up a dive mask with your mouth from the bottom of the pool, and then swim a hundred meters.

"Rescue Swimmer" was a really insulting evolution. The objective was to "rescue" one of the instructors from "drowning." Problem was, the instructor didn't really want to be rescued, which resulted in an all-out brawl in the deep end of the pool. This was the insulting part—you're trying to save the "victim" from drowning and he's beating the crap out of you. Being in the water increased stress, causing many guys to panic.

The water aerobics didn't end with Drown Proofing and Rescue Swimmer. There were also timed, two-mile open-water swims with fins, which sounds easy enough on paper, but if you've spent all day getting physically hammered and are dead tired by the time you get in the water, this significantly increases the level of difficulty. Then there's Surf Passage and Rock Portage. It sounds like the name of a seaside bar, but in reality, it's a damn challenging evolution: I once saw a guy break his leg doing it. The objective of Surf Passage was for our team to paddle our small rubber boat through the breaking surf out to open water. The instructors would wait until the waves were just right—big, noisy, and frequent—and then they would send us into the fray. It was a mess: boats would spill guys out and flip over, and the currents would wash us right back to shore after the waves pounded and spun us around. Once a boat crew made it out to the open water, we would paddle back to shore over a shoreline piled high with huge rocks, enormous triangular slabs of granite. It seemed like every slab had hard, sharp, curb-like edges. They were woven together like a Chinese finger trap: where the cylinder locks around your finger when you try to pull it out. The granite slabs worked much the same way—you would be stepping between the rocks to get back to shore, and the slabs would lock you in place when you tried to pull your foot out. And if you were unlucky enough to get caught between the slabs while a wave was coming down, something was going to snap. Eventually our boat team made it over both the surf and the rocks unscathed after a few hard attempts.

BUD/S demands that you find a way to remain calm under stress, because you have only two options: either keep going or quit. *Evolution* is the perfect term to describe these tests, as the goal is always to *evolve*, to be able to accomplish the next one. I have come to view all the challenges, hardships, and obstacles that I face in life as evolutions, much like the ones I went through in BUD/S and others in my SEAL career. Successfully completing one hard evolution prepares me for the next—and usually more difficult—ones. The degree of difficulty of each evolution demands that I focus only on the task at hand. This engagement with the present moment is timeless—there is no future or past to distract, only the here and now. That's how I made it through these tests, by being preoccupied by the present. I believe that my mission in this life is to evolve, and the most important people in my life are those who challenge me to do this.

Hell Week

Hell Week didn't come as a surprise to anyone. The Navy even put a notice in the local paper warning the public in advance of gunfire and explosions. It was a Sunday afternoon in the Southern California winter when 120 SEAL candidates gathered in a classroom and watched the movie *The Navy Frogmen*. After the movie, we all waited in the same classroom until about 11:00 p.m., when the instructors calmly informed us that Hell Week had begun. We lined up and walked out of the classroom, then jogged in formation over the sand berm to the beach behind our facility.

That's when all hell broke loose, and the shooting, explosions, and the intense physical activity began.

Hallucinations are a common and predictable occurrence during Hell Week. I had my first ever hallucination a few days in, during a fourteen-mile paddling excursion known as "around the world." San Diego Bay was glass flat, not a ripple on the water. I looked down and could clearly see hundreds of long silver fish all around me, bobbing up and down just below the surface, smiling at me. I asked the guy in front of me, "Hey, do you see all those fish?" When he didn't respond, I figured he was probably enjoying his own hallucination and had no idea what I was talking about. After the bobbing fish, my hallucination got even better; I then saw massive black squares cut out of the water. I was concerned that we were going to fall into one of them, but the squares always moved as we got closer.

SEALs are a creative bunch and would come up with all kinds of interesting mental and physical obstacles to put in front of us during Hell Week. There was an evolution called "Sol

Solly," where two ropes were strung over a muck pit located behind some sand berms, and our objective was to shimmy across this makeshift rope bridge about twenty-five yards to the other side of the muck pit without falling in.

The pit had a greenish hue and smelled like a cesspool. I turned sideways and placed both my feet on the lower rope. Directly above me was the top rope. I reached up and grabbed on, holding tight to keep my balance. I was wet, cold, hungry, and already covered in muck. I inched forward, making my way over the deep muck pit, when the instructors grabbed the ropes on either end and began rocking and swinging them, trying to dislodge me and dump me in—which they did. When Sol Solly ended, we all sat on the banks of the pit and ate macaroni salad out of plastic tubs with our muck-coated hands while the instructors threw grenade simulators in the water, flinging more muck on us. Getting the chance to be stationary for a few minutes was awesome. We just had to eat some mud to pay for it.

Camp Surf

I can't remember a time I was ever as cold as I was during the Hell Week evolution called "Camp Surf." The instructors built a huge campfire on the beach and we all sat around it and were made to tell a joke or story. After the storytelling ended, we were directed to go lie in the fifty-five-degree water, then crawl in the sand and attempt to sneak past the instructors up to the campfire to warm up. It was really challenging, as there were lots of instructors stationed between the water and the fire. The objective was not to get caught, or we'd be sent back into the ocean to do it all over again. The cold, wet sand and plants that covered the dunes were coated with ice; they both sucked all the heat from my body, and I cramped up everywhere. At one point, a guy lying next to me in the surf zone asked if I wanted to quit with him. I sat up and looked around. I believe he thought by that movement that I was going with him. He immediately stood up and started walking to the bell. About halfway there, he looked over his shoulder at me as I lay back down in the surf. I don't remember his name, but I do remember the look of complete shame and disappointment on his face. I didn't do it to trick him, but those things did happen. He was one of many that the Camp Surf evolution broke. I had had far more difficult experiences in life and was still very far from my breaking point.

Quitting was simple during Hell Week. Instructors would constantly ask, sometimes quite loudly, "Do you want to quit?" Usually, this offer also came with the temptation of hot cocoa, doughnuts, and a nice, warm, comfy place to enjoy some of the Navy's delicacies. This is referred to as Drop on Request (DOR). If someone replied in the affirmative, he would drop his BUD/S helmet next to a pole on the quarter deck with a brass ship's bell attached to it and ring it three times, and just like that he'd be on to a new career.

I was nearly rolled back again during Hell Week. Somehow, I had managed to rip a deep hole in the back of my leg. The Hell Week doctor was concerned that I would contract some type of flesh-eating bacteria. I asked to keep going, and the medical staff shot me up with antibiotics and sent me back in. Then the sun rose on Friday morning, and I had a sense that I was going to make it.

In the afternoon, the instructors started in on us like it was the first night of Hell Week all over again. That's the only time I ever questioned what I was doing, putting myself through this prolonged, voluntary torture session. But almost as soon as the beatdown started, it abruptly ended, and we were directed to march over a sand berm where the command staff stood waiting for us. We circled the staff and took a knee; the commander offered a brief congratulations, and we were officially secured.

I had completed Hell Week. Brenda, my then-girlfriend and soon-to-be wife, took care of me for the next few days. I couldn't talk, my feet were so swollen that I could only wear flip-flops, the hole in my leg was still healing, and my hair had rubbed off from the friction of continuously carrying around a rubber boat on my head. Brenda's care was foreign to me. She did everything she could to keep me comfortable and get me back on my feet, literally and figuratively, but I still wasn't used to being nurtured. It was nice to have someone in my corner for the first time.

Hell Week affects everybody in different ways. Most of the class quits by Wednesday, but then there are guys like Dave, one of my BUD/S classmates who finished Hell Week Friday afternoon, cleaned himself up, and went out drinking that same night like it was no big deal. There was another guy we nicknamed DMSO2 Bob. His rank was second class and he was an older guy in his mid-thirties. He was at the top of the class and a physical stud. He would rub DMSO—dimethyl sulfoxide, a chemical used in the horse racing industry and in veterinary medicine to treat horses with ligament issues—all over his legs and arms to help recover. Absorbing the DMSO through his skin day after day did have the unfortunate side effect of making his breath smell like fermented roadkill.

It was Wednesday night of Hell Week, two more days to

go, and we were all in the chow hall eating when DMSO2 Bob stood up and said, "There's raisins in my oatmeal." He walked over to the bell, rang it, and quit right there. This was DMSO2 Bob's second appearance at BUD/S, and from what I was told later, he had quit at the exact same time both tries, Wednesday night of Hell Week. After Wednesday night, everybody is sort of on autopilot and the physical intensity and harassment level drops off, or maybe we just got better at ignoring it. Bob was one of the best athletes in the class. He just couldn't break through that barrier of Wednesday night.

Everyone has flaws and weaknesses, and Hell Week highlights them to an extreme some people's systems can't handle. The Navy now offers counseling to those who wash out of BUD/S, a change that was instituted after one unsuccessful candidate died by suicide. I can see how BUD/S can cause trauma or trigger it, or how failing it can lead to an extreme reaction. There is no shame in not completing BUD/S. While I served as a Navy SEAL and really enjoyed my career, it was my job, not my identity.

But Hell Week is not the end of BUD/S. In fact, the hard part had not even started.

Second Phase: Land Warfare

I turned nineteen years old during Second Phase. Brenda made me cupcakes and had them sent out to San Clemente Island where we were training. What Brenda didn't know, unfortunately, was that the absolute *last* thing you want is to let anyone in the SEAL community know it's your birthday, or any occasion where you can be singled out. The cupcakes were sent with a note on the box that read: *Since it's Mike's Birthday, don't be so mean to him.* The instructors pulled me aside and made me do a few hundred push-ups. They ate most of the cupcakes and sent me on my way. They were just messing with me and it was kind of funny. I think I ate one cupcake.

Land warfare was where we learned how to blow stuff up. I was nineteen years old and being trained on how to use some of the most powerful explosives ever created. Kind of hard not to have fun. We would swim out and attach explosives to these old WWII–era, X-shaped boat obstacles and then blow them sky-high out of the water. We used all types of explosives and blew up all sorts of stuff—every day was like the Fourth of July. We also got some very basic training in different weapon systems and marksmanship. There was a land-navigation course that was damn hard, and a whole bunch of other training like rappelling and small-unit tactics.

We slept in big aluminum-covered huts. One night, we had a biblical rainstorm that lasted a few days, flooding the huts. Instead of blowing stuff up, we spent days bailing ourselves out of the water and digging irrigation drains that led down to the beach. I think the Navy has since made a few infrastructure improvements to the accommodations on the island.

San Clemente is uninhabited except for a few hundred Navy visitors. The lack of people makes the waters around the island superb for swimming and diving. We would do four-mile swims through massive kelp beds where we'd encounter all kinds of marine life, including the other kind of seals, the occasional dolphin, and sharks.

These swims got me in great shape for the upcoming dive phase. We had to complete a timed two-mile ocean swim with fins in seventy-five minutes, and by this point it was easy. There was another four-mile timed run with boots that you had to finish in twenty-eight minutes and forty seconds, and later a fourteen-mile run in soft sand.

Third Phase: Combat Diving

The final phase of my BUD/S tour was the Dive Phase. My father may have provided me an advantage here—most of the diving that I did in Third Phase was in cold black water with almost zero visibility. I had already been conditioned to this experience years before, when my father would make me dive into and scour creeks and ponds around our New Jersey home for drunk peoples' lost wallets. That was where I'd learned to relax and hold my breath for long periods of time and get comfortable in the water. It was the perfect training to inoculate me against the fear of diving into the cold, dark unknown.

A few guys in my class made it through both Hell Week and Land Warfare only to wash out during Dive Phase. These candidates had one last chance to pass, or they were sent back into the fleet. Jumping out of planes was the second most technical and dangerous job I had in the Navy; diving was the first. There is zero room for error in diving, where problems can turn catastrophic in a split second. Skydiving and combat diving are very much alike in this way.

Remaining composed under pressure and calmly working through various problems is the only way to survive these situations, because panic can be a death sentence. Dive Phase offered a new layer of stress that tested and trained me to remain calm in chaotic situations. "Combat diving" is the perfect name for it, because at times it was more like fighting underwater while trying to breathe than diving. The evolutions were designed to be extremely uncomfortable, but not kill us. We played violent games of six-on-six underwater hockey; at one point, someone bit my leg. I could hold my breath for four minutes, which was a huge asset, because I had more time to figure things out underwater before the panic reflex of not being able to breathe kicked in.

Dive Phase is where I was introduced to open-circuit scuba and closed-circuit diving using a rebreather. Most people are familiar with the open version—tanks on your back filled with air that releases bubbles as you exhale. In the closed version, you use a rebreather that recycles your exhaled gasses, which you can then rebreathe. The LAR V rebreathers we use in the SEAL teams are made by Dräger and are often referred to as "Drägers." These were the same type of rebreathers used by German frogmen during World War II.

The difference between SEALs and other Special Forces divers is that we train to swim and dive as a means of long-range transportation to and from our intended targets. This means that we need to be comfortable in hostile environments so we can get to a target and do our jobs. After a while, the water became my safe place; I felt more at peace in the water than I did on land. I still do.

I have found that some of the best ways to overcome fear, instill confidence, and build resiliency is to seek out and do the uncomfortable. For me, activities like diving, skydiving, and fighting people I knew could whip my ass purged my fears to the point that I became comfortable and confident in those settings. The confidence gained from these activities and ability to remain calm under stress carries over into other parts of life too. I didn't understand it at the time, but stress, like working out, builds psychological resiliency. Over the years, I have had many opportunities to develop resiliency as my response to heavy doses of both physical and psychological stress. My response to stress is to control only what I can, know what is out of my control, and not expend too much energy on either. I only really have control over how I frame and react to every situation in my life. I have come to learn that when I'm in control of my emotions, I can better evaluate stress and find small ways to improve my situation, which gives me some level of control.

Human Obstacles

BUD/S candidates are all paired up with swim buddies. It's an unusual concept: the Navy's equivalent to creating a Siamese twin. There is no civilian counterpart to a swim buddy. You become each other's full-time lifeguard, instant best friend, and wingman for all occasions. It was the first time that I ever remember having anyone in my life who was fully responsible for my well-being, my location, and my safety. Like Siamese twins, you never, ever leave your swim buddy's side. When my swim buddy was sent to lie faceup, fully clothed in the Pacific Ocean while cold surf washed over him, I was right there by his side in the water. He was beside me when I was instructed to get wet and sandy. We ran, walked, crawled, swam, froze, ate, drank, and did everything by each other's side. We struggled together, which somehow made the experience slightly more bearable and at times almost fun. Most of these BUD/S candidates did not make it past the first few weeks. Thus, I had a dozen or more swim buddies. I can't remember all of their names, but I do recall that each one added something extremely positive to my BUD/S experience; just knowing that I could count on them helped me get through the process.

God forbid if any of us ever wandered too far from our swim buddy. This was a serious offense, and the punishment was severe. The command's message was clear: stick together, you are responsible for each other, and work as a team. This is also a leadership exercise: You lead by taking care of others. You don't need authority to do it. This practice makes everyone a leader, in tune with the needs of others, always observing, always working together, and always seeking to improve.

Every BUD/S class starts with over a hundred guys. Many come into BUD/S with more testosterone and arrogance than willpower. In my experience, the guys who were the best athletes and perfect physical specimens were typically some of the first to quit. Bentley was the exact opposite of these guys. He was the toughest guy in my BUD/S class. At about five foot nothing, and bone thin, he would not quit, no matter what the instructors did to him. They made him sit in a rubber boat while we carried him around the base chanting, "Hail Bentley, King of the Shit Birds," but he took the humiliation like a champ and still refused to ring the bell. Finally, the instructors told him that he was too small and was going to get hurt. They kicked him out. But Bentley broke *them*—he beat BUD/S! He had more heart than all of the perfect physical specimens, who quit way before he was forcibly removed. Some thirty years later, I still remember Bentley because of his heart. He just refused to quit. I don't remember any of the names of the perfect physical specimens who quit.

Dive Phase included timed, open-water swims of two nautical miles, three and a half nautical miles, and five nautical miles; this distance works out to be a seven-statute swim. Each of these was required to pass BUD/S. Ron, my swim buddy, was tough as nails, a solid athlete and a strong swimmer. We entered the water together and swam side by side for six of the seven miles. This was when I noticed that he was slowing down, and then he stopped moving altogether. You never, ever, leave your swim buddy. Now we were stopped dead, bobbing in the water a full nautical mile from the finish line in the freezing open ocean. His legs had just quit working, no kick; he was shivering and had turned a beautiful shade of light blue. Our options were:

1. drown together, which would mean that neither of us would graduate;
2. signal a safety boat and quit, which would mean that we both failed the swim and would have to do it all over again; or
3. figure out a way to finish the swim together before we both drowned or succumbed to hypothermia.

We decided on Option 3. I dragged us the last mile to the finish line. I know, if our roles had been reversed, that he would have done the same for me. When we arrived on dry land, my swim buddy was nearly unconscious from hypothermia. We finished the swim, but I later ended up having to do it all over again.

We were already close, but that swim forged a tight bond between Ron and me, especially that last mile. After thawing, we eventually both graduated BUD/S, him in class 168, and me several months later in class 169. He ended up the best man at my wedding.

Timed Run

Some of my greatest challenges at BUD/S were not the physical ones; rather it was navigating some of the personalities. I had one instructor, a junior officer, who accused me of stealing equipment. "Seaman Recruit Day, why do you have seven knives and four CO_2 cartridges in your locker?" I thought that he was just messing with me—it was one of the many kinds of mind games instructors played on us recruits.

I told him I didn't have seven knives and four CO_2 cartridges in my locker. He replied, "Then one of us is lying. Who is it?"

I responded, "Then it must be you, because I'm not lying."

From that point forward, I was a marked man and he ordered one of the other instructors to harass me constantly. I hadn't answered the officer's question with the intent on being disrespectful; I just didn't realize answering so matter-of-factly would be interpreted as discourteous.

I was nearing the end of the last phase of BUD/S and had already been rolled back from class 166 to class 168 for shin splints. Passing meant that I had to complete four-mile runs in soft sand wearing boots in twenty-eight minutes and forty seconds. I was completing the runs under the required 7:10 pace. Now this instructor was intentionally failing me on every timed run, no matter how fast I ran. One day, I hid a watch in my running shorts (we were not allowed to carry watches) and timed myself. I more than beat the cutoff time but the instructor failed me anyway. There were a half dozen guys behind me who also failed. I was punished with extra push-ups, sand berm runs, lying in the cold Pacific surf, and rolls in the sand to get wet and sandy.

I was getting my ass handed to me after each timed run and in any spare moment between other evolutions. I needed to take matters into my own hands if this harassment was to stop. I reached out to Doc Flynn, a SEAL instructor I trusted and told him that I had timed myself and I more than passed. He said that he would do the next run with me and keep pace. "If you beat me to the finish, you're good," he told me. The next day, I did the run and finished with about seven other guys. We all reached the end of the run well before Doc Flynn. The other instructor said that we failed when Doc Flynn came across the finish line and confronted the other instructor, saying we'd all passed.

There was a brief argument, but the harassment ended as a result. I was rolled back again into class 169 for missing the cutoff of the timed run, which meant that I would have to do it all over again, even though I'd passed. This was graduation week. Unlike my last graduation, this one meant everything to me. I had been rolled back once in boot camp and now twice in BUD/S. I cried in my room that night. While I didn't understand it at the time, crying is a part of resiliency. It's a normal emotional release valve, a way of purging built-up stress, much like working out. Both tears and sweat carry with them human stress chemicals in the fluids that exit our bodies. So, I cried, and woke up the next day ready to finish what I'd started.

Graduation Congratulations?

One of the strangest phone calls I ever received came a few days after I graduated BUD/S. This was back in the day when nobody owned a cell phone. I was still living in the BUD/S barracks on base and there was only one pay phone located on the first floor of the quarter deck. Someone came up to my room and said that I had a phone call. I had never received a call while in BUD/S and had no idea how anyone could get a number to a pay phone.

When I answered, I was shocked to hear my father's voice come over the phone. I had not seen or heard from him in seven years. It was a bizarre exchange—he rambled for a few minutes about nothing and then told me that he wished "the wind would blow through your hair and it all fall out." Oddly, my hair had fallen out—or, more accurately, it had been polished off by a rubber boat keel.

To this day, I have no idea how he got that number or how he knew that I was in BUD/S, let alone graduated. I think his comment came out of the fact that he had lost his hair, which really bothered him. He was very sick.

The Tribe

Successful SEAL candidates all knew how to endure endless hours of cold and unpleasant tasks. Some guys seemed to even take pleasure in both. They knew from experience that hard work and just plain old "sucking it up" trumped talent when it comes to long-term physical endurance. These guys weren't the biggest, strongest, tallest, or fastest, but they took care of each other; persevered despite the cold, pain, and exhaustion; and inspired others to do the same.

I grew up in the SEAL teams, was raised by this charming pack of wolves. What I miss most about the teams are the relationships. SEALs are a strange tribe, and being around the guys is always fun. I once read that the brain is a social organ that needs relationships to develop and is influenced by these relationships.* While we gave each other a hard time, we

---

* Dr. Louis Cozolino, a psychologist and neuroscientist at Pepperdine University, talks about the brain as a social organ and that it evolved to connect with other brains in "The Brain Is a Social Organ," https://sel.cse.edu/louis-cozolino-the -brain-is-a-social-organ/.

understood and took care of each other. It's not uncommon for SEALs and other service members exiting the military to find themselves feeling empty, stressed out, or bored living in the civilian world; at times I've felt all three. It takes time to build trusting relationships, find a new purpose, and create a support network. It took me nearly a decade after leaving the military to understand the value of these new relationships and support network. These external relationships helped fortify my much-needed internal resiliency.

Two weeks after BUD/S graduation, on September 7, 1990, I drove from San Diego to Fort Benning in Georgia, to attend jump school. I had never jumped out of a plane before. I checked into my hotel near Fort Benning and called my wife, Brenda, who told me that along with jumping out of an airplane, I could add fatherhood to my growing list of new experiences—she was pregnant. All at once I was nineteen, a new SEAL team guy, and a father-to-be.

The physical training I did in BUD/S gave me a considerable advantage at jump school, at least when it came to discipline. Instructors would dish out push-up punishments in quantities of ten. I had been doing hundreds of push-ups at BUD/S, many of them wearing scuba tanks, so ten push-ups felt more like a reward than a punishment.

I had to do my best to hide the fact that I was terrified at the thought of jumping out of a plane. I had a sense that my instructors may have known it—they had seen a thousand guys like me over the years: cocky, freshly minted Navy SEALs coming to learn how to jump out of planes with the regular Army recruits. We started with static line jumps out of a slow-moving plane with a bunch of other guys. This was basic parachuting; my job was to step out of the plane and land without injuring myself or anyone else.

I can't tell you what my first jump looked like, or the twenty jumps after that, because I had my eyes closed the whole time. The experience is much different when your eyes are open, because you can actually see the ground. Closing my eyes on exit kept me from seeing the opening sequence. I closed my eyes until I felt the parachute coming off my back, then I would open them and have a look around. On the static line jumps you tuck your chin and would see the ground speed by your feet as your parachute is being opened by the static line.

I eventually transitioned from static line jumps to free-fall jumps. The experience was the same with free fall—a lot more fun with my eyes open. I was still terrified, but the more I jumped, the more I enjoyed it. After a few weeks, and ten static line jumps, I managed to earn my jump wings.

SEAL Qualification Training (SQT)

On October 5, 1990, I graduated from jump school and was shipped off to the twenty-six-week SEAL Qualification Training (SQT) course. SQT is far more advanced than BUD/S, and it's where I would be introduced to close-quarters combat training. This training has changed significantly since, in part because of what happened to me.

I spent a few weeks up in Kodiak, Alaska, doing cold weather training before being sent back to California to attend Survival, Evasion, Resistance, and Escape (SERE) training school. SERE school began with classroom instruction, which led to hands-on application in each of the Survival, Evasion, Resistance, and Escape phases. Once the education part was complete, we were all sent out into a densely wooded area to hide for half the day. I took a nap under a bush until the pre-briefed signal—a siren—sounded to call us in from our hiding places during the Evasion phase. I took the nap because there was no way not to get caught. It was a lot like Camp Surf, but in the desert and during the day. Moving from one place to another through a highly channelized route without getting caught by the many instructors was nearly impossible. My buddy was a pilot who decided to go anyway. He got caught and started the SERE training a few hours earlier than me.

Eventually we were all rounded up for what was to be a short stay in our new home: a mock-up POW camp. My first minutes in this SERE phase were painful. The "guards" with their horrible fake Russian accents made us all line up, drop our pants, and spread our cheeks. "Spread them like you going to tear yourself in two!" they yelled. I just stood there; I wasn't dropping my pants. I had no idea that we were just going through a medical inspection—medical staff were looking for ticks and cuts that could become infected. This big guard walked up to me and told me to drop 'em. I refused. He then slapped me so hard he rocked me back on my heels. I saw stars. Through my daze, I heard the sound of zippers being ripped open and belt buckles hitting the ground. I staggered back to attention, then dropped my pants and presented an expanded view of my buttocks. Apparently, the camp anal inspector really liked what he saw: no ticks, cuts, or anything else that would threaten my continual stay in his fine school.

Another guard who had it in for me would come into my cell, pick me up, and fling me against a metal wall. He did this a few times, until I would just go totally limp in his arms. He didn't want to go through the effort of lifting me up to chuck me, so he left me alone. Feigning weakness had its benefits.

SERE was just another in a long series of tests, and like all the others, I'd passed.

CHAPTER 5

SEAL Team 3—Surf Reports

After completing BUD/S and SEAL Qualification Training in early 1991, I was assigned to SEAL Team 3, a West Coast team. Even-numbered teams are stationed on the East Coast in Virginia, and odd number teams are based in San Diego, California. I liked California and was happy to stick around.

Back in the 1990s, everyone had a six-month probationary period before your fellow teammates would recommend that you receive your Warfare insignia. Only then would your SEAL team commander issue you your Trident. There was so much crazy hazing back when I went through the process; nowadays, what we did to each other would be considered assault. The Navy has cracked down on hazing, but it still happens in the teams. It's all in good nature and humor. They are meant to be rites of passage to affirm that you are accepted and trusted. We could always pick out the guys who wouldn't be around long, and they were not hazed.

We were finishing up some dive training in Washington State when the guys decided to initiate me into the club. They stripped me totally naked, duct-taped me so that I couldn't move, then spray-painted me black everywhere except my face. Yes, they even spray-painted my groin, which burned. As if that wasn't enough, they then dipped me in the forty-degree Puget Sound. These were my friends. Apparently, I passed the initiation rite, because when we arrived back in San Diego, the platoon officially recommended me to the commander to earn my Trident and I officially became a Navy SEAL.

The SEAL teams are full of traditions, and one of them is the "punching in" ceremony. The Navy SEAL Trident is worn on the left side of your chest above all other devices. There were six or seven of us coming onto Team 3. The Trident is a big device and is attached to the uniform with three needle-like prongs that fasten on the opposite side, much like a lapel pin. The commander welcomed me to the Navy SEAL community and placed the Trident in my hand. After he did the same to the others, the team guys lined up, and the first guy took your Trident and placed it on your chest, then pounded it into your body with his closed fist. The Trident's three prongs were then dug into your flesh.

Everyone on the team took their turn pounding our newly issued Tridents into our chests, one after the other. The commander was the last guy to pound in my Trident. He had a big grin on his face as he approached. He pulled the Trident out of my body and straightened it out like he was fixing a bent nail; then he placed it on my chest and slowly pushed it back in. *Damn!* That hurt way more than having it punched in.

Before we bury one of our own, SEALs remove their Tridents from their uniforms and pound them into their fallen brother's wooden casket. We are a close community—and you never, ever leave your swim buddy.

Surf Reports

My new skipper was a surfer—my job was to provide him with the official base surf report every morning at 0730. PT normally started at 0730 and ended at 0930. Our morning workouts consisted of body-weight exercises, swim-run-swim sessions on the beach, and/or a few laps through the O-course (obstacle course). My first attempt at the O-course in BUD/S took me forever. The O-course consisted of a series of obstacles that included jumping from stump to stump, climbing and sliding down ropes, climbing elevated obstacles and walls, and crossing rope bridges. When I arrived at Team 3, I could knock it out in a little over six minutes. On Wednesdays we had individual PT, which meant surfing or volleyball. On mornings when the surf was favorable, the skipper would send me out to check the surf report, and if it looked favorable, he would cancel our regular morning PT and all us surfers, including the skipper, would go ride waves for a few hours. The other guys would be on their own and do individual training.

The skipper was the first of three Irish American commanders that I had while with Team 3. Different nationalities are known for their specialties: the Swiss have cheese and neutrality. The Irish have thick dark beer, strong whiskey, and fighters. The Irish are well represented in the SEAL teams.

The skipper was a badass. He would give all the young guys a run for their money on the O-course; he would beat guys half his age, and he could surf. The commander also knew how to stay close to the guys he led. He would be right beside us in the surf; in most cases, he was in front of us leading PT or any other kick-in-the-nuts training exercise. He had an incredible memory and knew all of our names, our wives' names, and our kids' names. You could tell he loved us and was proud of us. He led by example, kept us focused, and did his best to protect us from ourselves.

Dive Hazards

I did a good deal of diving with Team 3. Diving is like entering a different universe, one where all the rules of dry land—like gravity, breathing air, and normal atmospheric pressures—don't apply. Diving is like traveling in outer space, so much so that NASA uses a pool simulator to train astronauts. You are in another world when you are underwater. Unless you came equipped with gills to separate O_2 from H_2O, you will need to learn how to breathe underwater.

Once you have mastered this task, then you need to learn how not to kill yourself from diving too deep and coming up too fast, which can cause decompression sickness (DCS), otherwise known as "the bends" or "Caisson's disease." Most dive-related ailments are caused by abrupt changes in pressure. The Navy created Dive Tables that give divers parameters as to what depths and dive times are more or less safe.

Dave, one of our senior guys, was a dive master and an under-the-sea guru. He was fifty-three years old when I met him—a total stud, strong as a bull, all muscle and 1 percent body fat. Dave was built like a Greek god. He had so little body fat that you could watch his muscle fibers and veins working under his skin. The Navy had a body fat formula and wanted to kick him out because he didn't meet a random body fat percentage ratio or some other nonsensical requirement. We sent them a picture of Dave shirtless and they reenlisted him.

Dave was everyone's dive mentor; he was so comfortable and confident in the water, he was like a damn merman. One day, he failed to return from a solo recreational ocean dive and we went out looking for him. We found him three days later still wearing all of his dive gear, clutching his attack board, regulator still clenched in his teeth. He had passed away from a massive heart attack. Diving is dangerous business. Dave's death was calibrating; he was our "indestructible" role model. He was also human and mortal. That realization meant that I had to recognize my own mortality and accept the possibility of dying on the job.

There are so many hazards in the water and so many things that can go wrong during a dive. One ping from a ship's sonar can blow off a diver's mask and knock him unconscious. Ship water intakes and discharges can wreak havoc on a dive plan. One night, my dive buddy and I were doing a training dive in San Diego Bay when I decided to come up and have a peek. We broke the surface and saw a tugboat headed straight for us. A tug's propeller extends straight down under the boat. We flipped back under and swam like crazy to the bottom of the bay just in time for the prop to pass over us. I could feel the whirling blades of the propeller pass directly above me.

I was always more concerned about being hit by a ship than I was of being eaten by a shark while diving. It's not true that all Navy SEALs love the water; we had plenty of guys who hated it, but they put their disdain and fear aside and did it anyway because it was part of the job. I still consider diving the most dangerous task in the SEAL teams.

Swimming Against Dolphins

One of the most stressful training exercises I experienced was swimming against dolphins. The Navy uses dolphins to detect combat swimmers in open water and bays—they find the swimmers, ram them with a rubber cone attached to their snout, and then push the divers to the surface. They're basically three-hundred-fifty-pound swimming guard dogs.

For the training exercise, my swim buddy and I used a closed-circuit diving apparatus. We had to get all the way across the San Diego Bay without being dolphin-detected. Suddenly, out of nowhere, I got rammed by what felt like a small car. It hit me hard in the ribs and pushed me up to the surface. That damned dolphin would not leave me alone—he kept poking me with his nose cone and he looked like he was having fun. Those big "fish" pack a punch; it really did hurt. We got detected and had to do it over again.

It's Not Just a Job—It's an Adventure

The Navy aired a recruiting commercial that showed all sorts of cool stuff—guys flying off aircraft carriers, working the periscope in a submarine, scuba diving—and at the end of the spot, a man's voice said, "The Navy: it's not just a job, it's an adventure."

In my case, it was actually true.

My peacetime deployments took me around the globe, across Asia and the Middle East: Egypt, Kuwait, Japan, Korea, Guam, and points beyond and in between, conducting joint country-to-country training. On my deployment to Bahrain, we patrolled the Persian Gulf, enforcing oil embargos. We would board oil tankers that were in violation of various infractions— most of the time, the infraction was that they didn't identify themselves because their radio didn't work. We would catch tankers bearing the Iranian flag filled with embargoed Iraqi oil; there were all sorts of shenanigans going on.

The first few times we boarded a tanker were exciting, running across decks and cutting our way through steel hatches with torches, but after a few months it became routine. We were more like water cops than SEALs. And you'd think those massive tankers would be stacked with crew, but they usually only had a handful of guys. I think the most I ever counted was ten. The Navy eventually created Visit Board Search and Seizure (VBSS) teams with its fleet sailors to execute lower-level noncompliance issues.

Years later some folks figured out that these tankers were shockingly easy prey because of their small crews and lack of protection. Modern-day pirates had started seizing and ransoming oil tankers and commercial boats. When it was reported that a tanker had been hijacked off the coast of Somalia and its American crew was taken hostage, a team of my fellow SEALs was called in to take care of the problem. They successfully neutralized the hostage takers and rescued the American hostage. The event was recounted in the film *Captain Phillips*, starring Tom Hanks. Nowadays, you'll find retired team guys sailing on tankers around the world, providing security against pirates.

On most deployments, I would bring my surfboard and explore the local surf scene during my free time. I especially enjoyed my deployment to the Philippines, where I could grab my board and hitch a Jeep ride to the coast. The Jeeps would always break down, though, so the trips took a while. But once I got to the coast, I would find a boat to take me to an outlying island where everyone surfed. The surfing was sweet—clear blue water, long waves, easy breaks. There wasn't much out there, but every now and then someone would catch a big tuna, and we would all eat sushi and drink beers after a full day on the waves.

The Philippines was one of the most fun deployments I went on as a SEAL; it's also where I had my most terrifying dive experience, quite possibly one of the scariest events of my life. Every dive happens in pairs, with one driver and one navigator. I was the navigator on this training dive; my driver was a senior guy, Logan Hardgrave, who had a wealth of experience. I'd learned from Dave's death that just because a guy is experienced doesn't mean he's invincible or infallible. When we are underwater on the move, navigating by compass and time, we refer to this mode of submerged travel as "flying," because it is very much like flying a plane.

It was nighttime, pitch dark. Logan and I were swimming in black water. We were on our way to our target—a ship docked in one of the Philippines' million harbors. We were flying through the black cold Pacific with zero visibility. When we arrived on the assumed target, we found nothing. We felt around for a while, hoping to bump into our target, but nothing. I was sure we were off the mark. We needed to surface to take a peek. When we got to the surface, there was no surface: we banged our heads against a steel pier, and we were stuck under it.

I had been in some very tight spots before, but I had never experienced claustrophobia until that moment. We were surrounded by 360 degrees of blackness; we were lost, sucking up our O_2; and if we didn't regain our bearings fast, we'd circle under the pier until we ran out of air. I was scared, and really pissed off at my driver: we were a team, but it was his job to get us on the target. But there was no way to talk to each other and we couldn't see each other, so hand signals were useless. I suspected he was panicking too. I attempted to relax while I checked off each one of the emergency procedures. During periods of high stress, our autonomic nervous system takes over and our fight-or-flight response kicks in. I had to control, more like override, my body's automatic physiological response to extreme fear. I had to control my breathing, heart rate, and thoughts that were creating the fear. I had to put aside the concern of my possible death and work through the process of getting out from under the pier. This episode and others like it have helped to build my resiliency portfolio. They placed me at my physical or psychological limit and induced so much stress that I literally had to sink or swim. Successful navigating of these high-stress situations builds resiliency, a strong sense of self-reliance, and the skills and confidence to meet and overcome the next test.

It took us thirty minutes, but we eventually found the end of the pier by following seams and were able to surface. We returned to base, calmed down for a bit, then yelled at each other.

Just another test.

CHAPTER 6

Leap Frogs

It was 1996 and I was stationed in San Diego. I had just finished my fourth peacetime deployment with SEAL Team 3. I had been to multiple locations in the Middle East, North Africa, and Southeast and Southwest Asia, including the Philippines, Japan, Korea, Thailand, Singapore, Egypt, Bahrain, UAE, Kuwait, and Guam.

Deployments are hard on everyone, including our families. We work six, often seven days a week, sixteen hours a day in preparation to move men and equipment around the globe. We're away for six months only to return for a few weeks, unpack, do laundry, and then we leave to do it all over again. I had not been home much up till this point. I averaged three hundred to three hundred twenty-five days a year on the road while with SEAL Team 3. I was constantly having to get reacquainted with my own family after every long trip. My oldest daughter had been born before my first deployment. I did three more. I missed seeing my daughter's first steps and her first everything. I missed every holiday and birthday. I wanted more time with the ones I loved.

After my fourth deployment, I requested and received orders to report to BUD/S as an instructor. The BUD/S instructor assignment would have kept me home in California with my family for three whole years.

While my new orders were being processed, I was offered another option: I could try out for the Leap Frogs, the Navy's demonstration skydiving team. At that point, I had only logged thirty-five jumps. I showed up at the jump site with about fifteen other guys, all of them from different SEAL teams from either coast. Once we were all gathered and ready, we did a series of jumps, which proved to me that I had no idea what I was doing when it came to demonstration parachuting. It was fun to get the free training jumps using the Leap Frogs' "cool guy parachutes," but I was certain that I would not be selected for the team and would end up being a BUD/S instructor. The team trainer had recognized my lack of grace in the sky, but he also must have seen my hidden potential as a skydiver. He ended up picking me along with five or six other guys for the team. I'll never forget his response to my disbelief at being selected: "If I had enough bananas, I could teach a monkey to fall out of a plane." I think he meant it as a compliment.

He had over five thousand jumps at the time and told me about how even he'd had some trouble flying his first sixty or seventy jumps. Leap Frog parachute training has advanced since that old Frog had been shown how to put on a parachute and jump into the sky. The Leap Frogs regularly pushed the limits of skydiving and parachuting technology. We were innovators in canopy relative work (CRW) maneuvers and helped create and perfect some of the tricks and equipment used by sport skydivers today. Of all the jobs I've had as a SEAL, Leap Frogs was the most fun and beat me up the most. In 1996, we were a fifteen-man team of SEAL operators. Today, the team is open to SEALs, Special Warfare Combatant-Craft (SWCC) crewmen, and basically anyone in the Navy who is military free-fall qualified.

The whole "jumping out of a plane" thing is not the dangerous part of skydiving—opening the parachute and returning to earth safely, that's where things can get complicated. When you're free-falling to earth, you are basically an aircraft subject to all the same conditions as any other aircraft—pressure changes, turbulence, and of course gravity. Moving your body into the proper arch position while falling at high speeds takes extensive training, but once you get comfortable and relax, it's just like riding a bike—you just do it.

There are two different ways to fall out of an aircraft: static line or free fall. A static line jump is when you are attached to a static line while you exit the plane and the connected chute is automatically deployed when pulled by the line attached. I've accumulated a total of seventy-eight static line jumps. A free-fall jump is exactly that: you free-fall out of some type of airborne vehicle—a plane, a glider, a helicopter, even a hot air balloon— and you pull the chute yourself. Static line jumps remove some of the chute deployment risk; however, there is always the possibility of a "jumper-in-tow" incident, which happens when a static line does not pull the parachute off the jumper's back, resulting in a jumper being towed behind the aircraft. This is a horrifying scene, in which the jumper is tangled up outside the aircraft and is typically being slammed against the side of the plane as the crew desperately works to pull the jumper back in. Cutting the static line would release the jumper, but he would have to deploy his reserve parachute; however, the jumper may have lost consciousness from being slammed against the side of the plane. If the jumper can't get free, the pilot has to land the plane with the jumper attached.

I did meet a person who survived a jumper-in-tow event where the plane landed with him attached to the outside. I'm grateful that I never experienced that kind of malfunction; however, I had a few others that were scary enough. The Leap Frogs were a Free Fall and Canopy Relative Work team. My first two cutaways happened jumping over Key West, Florida, and they were violent. A main chute cutaway is exactly what it sounds like: you pull a handle and release your main parachute from your body. Once that's gone, all you have is your reserve chute. On my first-ever cutaway, we all got out of the plane clean and were building a stack—a vertical, chimney-like formation—in a fifty-mile-per-hour gust with 180-degree wind shear. We were in a seven-man stack doing rotations off the top to the bottom when we hit a terrible wind shear. The guy above me got his feet stuck in my risers; we twisted up and I got tangled in the chutes. These wind shears turned out to be pretty common at altitude in Key West. It felt and looked like two enormous hands compressed the top parachute all the way to the bottom one. The seven-man stack quickly turned into a falling mess of partially inflated parachutes, all going in multiple directions. It was a snarled mess; a couple of guys got shot out of the scrum and their parachutes reinflated. While we were all falling toward earth, another guy and I had to crawl out from under canopies to clear air space in order to cut away. I can't say exactly how fast we were falling, as there were fully and partially inflated parachutes, but even slowly falling out of the sky can be deadly.

I was still recovering from the terror of my first cutaway when my second happened a few days later. Me and another guy got tangled up and caught in a helicopter spin. The deployment bag retraction system on the tops of our parachutes had somehow gotten tangled together. We were twirling around opposite each other, falling. He was looking directly at me and I at him, and we yelled back and forth at each other, "CUT AWAY!" "NO! YOU CUT AWAY!" Like the world's most high-stakes game of rock-paper-scissors, he won and I cut away. I distinctly recall time slowing down during these episodes, exactly like what I would experience in that small room in Iraq years later.

It was after that second cutaway the guys on my team gave me the nickname "Cut-Away-A-Day." I now have just over twenty-three hundred jumps with a total of eight cutaways; I know guys with over five thousand jumps who don't have any. I guess I'm just lucky.

I had two very embarrassing landings. The first one happened in San Diego. The landing zone was a pier, and all the other guys nailed theirs. I was coming in on my final approach and was running out of pier, so I hooked hard at the last minute and landed in the water beside the pier. Everyone knew that it wasn't planned, but at least only my pride was wounded. The second one was at a Little League opening day game. I was flying into the diamond headed toward the pitcher's mound; everything looked great, until I got a little too close to the backstop. As I came in for the landing, my chute got all wrapped up on the top of the backstop. Nailed it—the backstop, not the landing. Everyone knew that that one wasn't planned either.

A parachute works just like the wing of an aircraft. The performance and reaction of the parachute are subject to air turbulence, just like an aircraft. We would often jump into stadiums and between buildings where air currents would be blocked and air turbulence could get pretty nasty, or the wind would enter in one location and would swirl in circles around a stadium, creating a whirlpool effect. These jumps were extremely dangerous. Once, we jumped into a Medal of Honor event in

South Carolina—our landing zone was located at the center of a group of buildings. I made it down to earth fine, but some of the other guys were coming in fast and hard, landing within twenty yards of me. Apparently, in that one location, the buildings cut off air flow, creating a dead spot. The buildings created wind eddies and bad turbulence. These obstacles can make parachutes fly like they have a mind of their own. One of our last teammates was on his final turn when he pulled his chute brakes to slow his descent, but instead of slowing down, he appeared to speed up. From the ground, I watched him pull on his toggles with no reaction from the parachute. He accelerated and then slid parallel to the earth across a road directly into a concrete street curb. I was ten feet away and watched both his legs snap like sticks. He should have been able to slow his forward air speed and land gracefully, but there was no response from the parachute other than to fly faster. His feet hit the curb at high speed; the impact crunched his legs and sent him into a violent somersault. He rolled a couple times and landed hard on his back. It was a gruesome injury; I will never forget the sound of his bones snapping on the cement. Everyone at the event saw it happen, and within thirty seconds he was surrounded by a dozen Medal of Honor recipients of every generation. Those guys sprang into action without a second thought, just like they were back on a mission. We got the guy to the nearest hospital, where he was put back together with pins and rods in both legs and feet. He ended up with thirty fractures in each leg from his knees down to his toes! A year to the day of the injury, that same guy was out jumping again like the injury had never happened.

My fellow teammates always seemed to be able to recover from all manner of injuries and traumas and get back in the saddle without any visible fear. I can't speak for my fellow team-mates, but I experienced plenty of fear, and I did what was necessary anyway. Surrounded by my fellow SEALs, I always had strong examples to follow.

There are other dangers when it comes to skydiving. Opening a parachute while falling to the ground at 120 miles per hour—terminal velocity—can result in what is known as a hard opening, which is a sudden hard jolt. There are other factors, including air speed, how the lines are stowed, and how the parachute is packed that can contribute to hard openings. If the parachute is not well organized when it's packed, it's not going to reorganize itself properly when it comes out.

I've had my fair share of hard openings. A "mild" one will clear your sinuses by knocking the snot out of you. I had a hard opening on a reserve parachute deployment that ripped my pectoral muscle from its connection point in my arm. I landed safely, then went and had both muscles surgically reattached to the bone.

According to the Navy, the primary mission of the Leap Frogs' Navy Parachute Team is to help Naval Special Warfare recruit qualified candidates. The Navy has multiple recruitment programs that have a similar goal, but those often miss their mark; however, I can honestly say that the Leap Frogs promotions really worked. I know that I am personally responsible for at least one successful recruit, my half brother.

On a jump into Veterans Stadium in Philadelphia, my younger half brother Sean—who I had not seen in nearly sixteen years—was in attendance. I loved jumping into stadiums—this one was tall, and the winds were high that day. We all flew backward into the stadium, from one end all the way to the opposite end. We nearly ran out of stadium, but we managed to put down "in bounds."

After the Veterans Stadium performance, Sean came and found me. I didn't recognize him—the last time we'd seen each other, I was twelve years old and being shipped off to Maine and he was asleep in his crib. He told me that after seeing me jump, he wanted to be a SEAL. I helped him get connected with a recruiter, and sure enough, a few years later, he graduated from BUD/S and earned his SEAL Trident. Coincidentally, he would end up in the same BUD/S class as Clarkie and a few others who were with me the night I was wounded.

I'm sure that there are countless stories of people who were inspired to become SEALs after seeing one of our performances or meeting members of our team. We were tasked to be ambassadors and would frequently do public appearances.

Missouri was by far my favorite jump location. We would jump into Kansas City Chiefs games, and the street around the stadium would be shut down for block parties. The team owner loved us—he had an apartment in the stadium and would invite us to watch the game while he fed us and opened the bar. One of my most memorable jumps was in St. Louis. This jump was one of those "don't try this at home" types. We had been planning it for months, practicing nearly every day until we perfected the maneuvers. It was a clear day with only a few scattered clouds. We circled the target to get a closer look, and on our second pass we all jumped out in a tight group. The brown muddy waters of the Missouri River stretched as far as I could see, and beside the river on a big green patch of grass was St. Louis's famous Gateway Arch. We were about a mile above it when we deployed our chutes, then got in a formation stacked on top of each other; we twisted and turned into position so that our feet connected.

We built our canopies up into a vertical stack and were flying together attached as we approached the arch. We threaded the needle, flying through one side and out the other. It was cool looking down at my feet and seeing them connected to another parachute. I felt like we were one canopy rather than four; we had so much lift and control. The force and speed felt like flying a plane. On another jump into Kansas City, I flew past a big skyscraper with mirrored glass windows. As I passed by it, I saw my reflection in the windows floating down to earth. I literally shouted, "Hey, that's me!" at it, I was so surprised.

After the jumps, I would go to the local high schools and talk with the kids for hours. I most enjoyed going to the schools in the tougher parts of town. There were times when I'd be in a gymnasium full of a few hundred kids and I was the only white person. They were mostly silent as I stood in front of them being introduced. These were kids who were growing up much like I had. I had no planned speech; I would just start talking. I would share with them that when I was about their age, I was fortunate enough after being expelled from high school to enter the Job Corps program, which helped me get out of a very violent and dysfunctional family situation and allowed me to earn my GED. Talking with the kids was strange, as it often felt like I was talking to the younger versions of myself. I would hang around after and meet privately with small groups of kids, who would share their own experiences and ask me personal questions about my life and career, which I would answer honestly.

People who have experienced trauma tend to attract others who have experienced similar trauma, and the kids who visited with me would share snippets of their struggles. While some may have considered me a role model, I viewed my story as a kind of exit strategy—a plan to get away from family dysfunction and violence, find a job, and be part of a new family. I wanted them to know that they could turn bad experiences into strengths. You can't change what has happened to you, but our response to the trauma can be used to make us stronger, more equipped, more attractive, and more powerful.

I would do a skydive performance and then spend the next day with kids from the Make-A-Wish Foundation, and others from the Shriners Hospital burn centers. I always felt privileged to meet these kids; they were real warriors in the fight every day. Meeting these kids and sharing time with them was one of the aspects of the job that I missed the most.

CHAPTER 7

Kosovo, Body Parts, and Danger Close

After three years with the Leap Frogs, I was assigned to a new SEAL team with a "Real Job." While we refer to them as peacetime deployments, this is not altogether accurate. Somewhere in the world people are fighting. There are East vs. West proxy wars raging, or soon to be raging, around the globe every day. We call them peacetime deployments because the United States is not technically at war in the area. However, there may very well be a war going on, and this was the case in Kosovo in 1999. The landlocked country of Kosovo came about after the fall of the Soviet Union, which began in 1989, roughly about the time I was in boot camp. The former Soviet Union was comprised of a block of nations in Eastern Europe that included Yugoslavia, a gigantic land mass that bordered Italy to the north and Greece to the south and took up nearly the entire coast of the Adriatic Sea. Yugoslavia was broken up into several different countries based on their ethnic populations. Kosovo, whose population is comprised of mostly ethnic Albanians, was one of them. Most Americans are familiar with Bosnia, one of the other dozen countries that formed after the breakup.

Kosovo would be my first education in what humans are capable of doing to each other.

The mission was a six-month deployment in a battle space run by NATO (North Atlantic Treaty Organization). The Serbians and their Russian allies were fighting against the ethnic Albanians for control of the region, which was considered sacred to the Serbians. NATO was allied with the ethnic Albanian forces, and we were tasked with working with NATO to assist them in apprehending suspected war criminals and keeping an eye on the movements of the various warring factions. Kosovo was a real-world test: we would do seventy-two-hour special reconnaissance (SR) missions in rugged terrain full of natural and man-made threats. We did twenty-five SR missions in six months, averaging about one a week, with one day of prep, three days on, and a debrief on either end. It was a kick-in-the-butt deployment.

It was unlike anything I'd ever experienced before. We would hear movement behind us in the pitch dark and could tell they were crawling toward our hide site. We had been set up for two days on an overwatch mission in a wooded area. I was sure that someone had seen us and now they were moving in to spray us with bullets or try to capture us. Normally we would take turns sleeping in four-hour shifts, but now we were all wide awake, weapons ready, waiting to be overrun or shot. Whoever was out there was extremely disciplined—it could have been the Serbian militia, or maybe even the Russians. We listened for hours as they rustled around in the thick brush to our rear. My heart was pounding all night as I waited for them to ambush us. We finally got eyes on them at sunrise: there were about twenty of them, camouflaged in black and green. The biggest was about a foot long. They had worked all night to dig up our two days' worth of poo and were eating it. Turns out, it wasn't the Serbs or the Russians, but a troop of Hermann's tortoises. We had nearly gotten into a gun fight with a group of slow-moving, crap-eating reptiles. Apparently, Kosovo is full of them and other reptiles, including horned vipers, the most venomous snake in Europe. We located one of these horned vipers and took pictures with it.

At one point during the deployment, we got dropped off into what our EOD tech believed was a minefield. Land mines were everywhere in Kosovo. Our EOD guy came to the front and began gently leading our patrol, picking his way carefully across the ground, waving his metal detector back and forth. The whole time, we were hauling ninety-pound packs uphill at night and needed to get to our hide site (about twelve clicks away) before the sun came up. In twenty minutes, we had moved maybe ten feet. At that pace, we would never get to our hide site in time.

I put the EOD tech at the back of the line and told him we would give him a call if we needed him.

One time while hunkered down in our hide site, we watched a group of kids moving a herd of cows and goats toward us. The cows got too close and started eating the foliage from our hide site. One of our guys had to smack it on the nose and the cow reared back. The kids knew someone was in the bushes, and they circled the cows behind us and ran them through our hide. We were all dodging and punching cows. Luckily for us, the herd of cows spooked and backed out. We waited until the kids and cows disappeared, then packed up and scrambled out of there fast. About fifteen minutes later, we heard gunfire coming from the direction that we had just evacuated. We assumed the kids had alerted some adults with guns as to our presence, and they were now throwing rounds into our hide site.

On another SR, we set up on a hill watching a Russian checkpoint when a Russian chopper flew over us. We decided to pack up and leave. Not long after, as we were departing the area, a couple of mortars hit the hill. The rounds were not close enough to see the splash of dirt, but close enough for us to hear and feel the explosions. More than close enough to put a hustle in our step.

When we were not doing SRs out in the Kosovo bush, we were on the business end of NATO's intel-gathering operations. On these operations, we were tasked with tracking and picking up accused war criminals. On one SR, we reported pickup trucks at a secluded residence delivering and receiving large quantities of packages. When I returned to do the debrief, I was told that the boxes were filled with human organs, and the warehouse was a body parts factory. In 2010, the *Guardian* published an article titled KOSOVO PHYSICIANS ACCUSED OF ILLEGAL ORGANS REMOVAL RACKET.* Apparently, the practice continues even today.

---

* Paul Lewis, "Kosovo Physicians Accused of Illegal Organs Removal Racket," *The Guardian*, December 14, 2010, https://www.theguardian.com/world/2010/dec/14 /illegal-organ-removals-charges-kosovo.

CHAPTER 8

September 11, 2001

I reported to Naval Special Warfare Group Two Training Detachment or TRADET on September 8, 2001, in a new instructor role and would remain there for a little over two years until 2004. I taught air operations, including parachuting and helicopter insertion, as well as extraction techniques. I spent time in the departments that developed land warfare tactics and close-quarters combat (CQC) training. This was a new command, with the idea of providing the best training to the SEAL community. It was staffed mostly by guys like me with leadership experience. It was a good group, but I would have much preferred to stay with a team. Three days later, I'd really be wishing I was back at a team.

On the morning of September 11, I was cutting my lawn in Virginia Beach when my wife called out to me from the house and said a plane had just hit one of the World Trade Center buildings. My first thought was, *Well, someone is about to get fired.* She called out to me a few minutes later and said that a second plane had just flown into the second building. That's when I knew it was no accident. I suspected that the attack had its origin someplace in the Middle East. There were multiple indications prior to the 9/11 attack. We knew of Osama bin Laden (or Usama bin Laden, shortened to UBL) and that he founded al-Qaida in 1988. Abdul Hakim Murad was a Pakistani citizen arrested in the Philippines in January 1995. He was affiliated with al-Qaida and had plans to blow up U.S. airliners over the Pacific and fly planes into CIA headquarters or other federal buildings. In August 1998, bombs killed 224 people at the U.S. embassy in Kenya and Tanzania. Intel from as far back as 1998 knew that UBL was developing an attack in the United States. Then in October 2000 the USS *Cole* was hit by a suicide bomber while docked in Yemen. These are just some of the indications; we had been hit at U.S. embassies and other U.S. targets around the Middle East for years.

I finished cutting the lawn, then got on the phone with my chief. We all were making calls and wondering when we would need to be ready to go. I knew it would take time to identify specific targets and put together a launch plan. My role would not change all that much directly after the 9/11 attacks. We were always preparing and training for war. This is the DNA of the SEAL community; we train, test, improve, and train some more. Being a SEAL prior to 9/11 was interesting, as I watched the many ways that the SEAL teams evolved because of these attacks. Up to this point, all of our training was based on known knowns; prior operations were used as case studies to adjust and improve current training. The community was prepared for war, but nothing changes tactics like current real-world lessons paid in blood. Our guys started going after bad guys and some of ours were coming home wounded. The enemy found ways to defeat our IED defenses and we lost guys. AARs, or after-action reports, are generated after engagements. The AARs are honest, no candy-coating lessons learned and what was done well and what needed to be fixed. We used the AARs to constantly adjust our TTPs (training, tactics, and procedures) to beat the enemies' tactics. Those two years were a busy time, planning and preparing to bring the fight to the perpetrators.

I've been asked if I feared the enemy in Iraq and any of the other places where I've been deployed. The answer is always no: the vast majority of enemies I've encountered are undisciplined and poorly trained, and many are what I refer to as economic combatants, who fight as a means for survival rather than ideology. Given the opportunity and means, I think those economic combatants would choose to leave their country and start a new life elsewhere, if that was an option.

But the enemy in Iraq had the advantage of using our own rules of engagement against us. Rules of engagement are designed to protect noncombatants; they also benefit an inferior military force. Back during WWII, we had one rule of engagement: win. The enemy in Iraq wove themselves into the population, took random shots at us, and paid people to plant bombs in the roads. Most of the time the enemy was lucky; then again, when you can use an entire population to hide under and do your dirty work, you get lucky more often.

I'm just your normal, run-of-the-mill everyday Navy SEAL, and I was far better trained and prepared than the best of the best foreign fighters. We often joked that we were not that good; it was that everybody else sucked. The U.S. military has conventional forces that are better than nearly all other military "special forces." While we face some very serious threats, America is safe with these warriors on the watch.

CHAPTER 9

Ambushes and Miniguns

Central Iraq, 2005: SEAL Team 4

I had arrived in Iraq in late 2005 on what was to be my first of two deployments to the country. I was a little nervous flying into Baghdad International Airport (BIAP) the first time. My expectation was of the worst environment imaginable. On final approach into BIAP, we were instructed to put on our Kevlar helmets and body armor in case we were to take fire. The huge C-17 cargo aircraft went into an aggressive, very steep dive to avoid small-arms fire and possible ground-to-air missiles. On the ground, it was like the other military airports I had been through, but the difference was that this was Iraq and there was a war. We were picked up in buses and trucks to move our gear. We drove through the base to our compound, and the roads were lined with barriers. Navigation used graffiti on the walls—for example, "turn right at the Kilroy Was Here tag." Iraq didn't remind me of any other place that I had visited. I didn't love or hate anything about Iraq; I just wanted to work. We all did. I had just completed a training workup at SEAL Team 4 and was ready to apply violence of action to the enemy.

We were traveling into the Iraqi badlands in a convoy made up of a mixture of forces, including a few Navy SEALs and Army Special Forces operators. We were heavily armed and moving fast, at times near sixty miles per hour, which is blazingly fast for a fully loaded and armored vehicle with a big gun sticking out the top.

We were speeding down the road and slid into a left turn. As soon as we made the corner, we nearly smashed into a make-shift roadblock. We must have been moving too fast, as we caught the roadblock construction crew off guard, who still had their AKs strapped to their backs. Their friends had all taken up positions on the right side of the road and had their weapons trained on us, ready to shoot as we sprinted around the corner. In a split second, the construction crew found themselves in a very awkward position, pinned between us and their friends, who wanted to shoot us.

In the confusion, we managed to get the jump on them. The lead Humvee was equipped with a minigun, and the gun-ner had the reflexes of a mongoose. Forty feet away from the targets and their rifle-wielding friends, I had a front-row seat to the action when the gunner opened up on all of them. I had not seen a minigun in live combat before, so I was a little sur-prised by what happened next. (By the way, there is nothing mini about a minigun; it's a pedestal-mounted six-barrel rotary machine gun that shoots as many as six thousand 7.62 × 51 mm rounds per minute, and the bullet is about the size of a AAA battery.) Bullets spit so fast out of the six Gatling-style rotating barrels that it looked like a red laser beam and sounded like the mating call of some bizarre prehistoric bird—*burrrr, burrrr.*

The first volley of bullets hit one guy in the chest, and he prac-tically vaporized in a burst of red mist. As this was going on, about fifty yards up the road, another enemy fighter popped up and fired an RPG directly into the lead Humvee, the one that was firing the minigun. I couldn't see the RPG, but I saw the Humvee ten feet in front of me lift up, drop back down with a crash, and catch on fire. The gunner didn't even flinch—he just kept on shooting. In thirty seconds, the twenty-five or so ambushers—including the RPG triggerman—had all been killed and were all red piles of flesh spread all over the street. When it was over, we secured the area, salvaged what we could from the still-burning Humvee, and then destroyed it with a thermite grenade.

The minigun turned twenty-five human beings into shredded flesh in less than a minute. *That was quick,* I thought, and then I felt weird, because the next thought I had was, *That was awesome.* Awesome because we did not get killed, and because of the power of the minigun. This was the first time I had seen people in the process of dying, but it was not the first time seeing dead people. My life and training had prepared me for these situations. My constant inoculation to violence and stress made what would have been grotesque and unbearable to many an acceptable situation to me. My trauma had conditioned me to accept the unacceptable.

That's what war does—it changes the way you view the world.

I found no pleasure whatsoever in killing the enemy. However, this was an outcome of war. Everyone at some point was someone's child, but that thought is lost in war. The most profane aspect of war is that it deletes the humanity from humans.

I saw myself as part of a professional clandestine military community. My missions were all based on extensive intelligence gathering, constant vetting of sources, and the use of leading-edge technology to identify our targets. My team's direct-action missions were capture or kill. Most of the time we snatched our well-armed targets without firing a shot. These were great missions; we would gain useful intel from our captured targets.

While the other members of SEAL Team 4 were doing direct action mission and/or personal security details for diplomats and politicians, I was working with a combined group of intelligence specialists from several other branches of the military. Our efforts were mostly done behind the scenes, developing trusted relationships with a network of well-placed individuals. We were working to identify people who were supporting bomb builders and sniper trainers, and in many cases we did.

What I came to learn is that war is a combination of ideology and economics. War zones create employment opportunities for civilian populations unfortunate enough to be living in these areas. We employed people in lots of different occupations: cooks, cleaners, translators, drivers, security personnel, construction workers, office workers, and many other jobs. These were people with very few options, and they needed to feed their families. But the enemy employed people too: they paid kids to plant IEDs, transport weapons, and gather intelligence on our routines and troop movements. Many of these people did the work for the same reasons their neighbors worked for us: they needed to feed their families. They didn't adhere to a rigid ideology; they needed the same basic things we all do, like food, shelter, and security. I could just as easily have been born in Iraq, a desperate kid looking for work. We tried to offer people an alternative, one that gave them a sense of dignity and hope and options. The enemy had no interest in any of these things; if people refused to do their work, they would kidnap, torture, rape, and kill men, women, and children alike. I saw their methods firsthand in the videos we recovered and the bodies of the victims themselves. Frankly, it was hard for me not to hate the enemy.

Part II

TRANSFORMED

When it comes your time to die, be not like those whose hearts are filled with the fear of death, so that when their time comes, they weep and pray for a little more time to live their lives over again in a different way. Sing your death song and die like a hero going home.

—Chief Tecumseh

CHAPTER 10

Medevac

April 6, 2007, Northeast of Fallujah

Back in the enemy compound, when the shooting stopped, I was still on the floor lying on my left side. I pushed myself up to my knees. I don't remember hearing any of the gunfire, but now sounds began to register in my ears.

The two men who had stacked up directly behind me in my room-clearing train were our Iraqi scouts. The second man in our train took a round to his chest plate and it knocked him clear out into the foyer. Ironically that round may have saved his life. He'd originally been within an arm's length behind me as we'd entered the room. The third man in my stack had been shot as he entered the room—a 7.62 × 39 AK-47 round had smashed through his bulletproof chest plate. He had fallen dead in the doorway.

The chance factor was insane. Once fired, a bullet can be unpredictable. The internal milling of a gun's barrel causes bullets to spin in flight—some bullets will begin to tumble through the air at low speeds, while others are designed to tumble and cartwheel after hitting a target, which can cause some brutal damage. It's likely that we were all hit by the same type of bullets, at nearly the same time, shot from the same gun, but the damage to each of us was significantly different. The balance of my room-clearing train—five or six other guys—hadn't been able to get into the room at all because of the sheer volume of fire.

I moved from my knees and stood to my feet. It felt like there were two hundred pounds on my back. I took off my helmet and used the white light on my damaged pistol to survey the room. One of our other Iraqi scouts entered the room—he had been behind Clarkie and followed him into his room. The bullet that hit Clark bypassed all three of the Iraqi scouts stacked up behind him. These three made it into Clarkie's room and had gotten trapped in the back of the house when the shooting started. The scout had been part of the original group of ten recruits who had been with us since the first day. He spoke decent English and gave me a report: one SEAL killed in action (KIA), one Iraqi scout KIA, two detainees, and six women and children.

I needed to secure the building myself, so I moved into the foyer with its glowing lamp and then into the room directly beside where my gunfight had happened. There were the six women and children, all sitting in the far corner screaming and crying. I pointed my white light at them and yelled, "SHUT UP!" None of them spoke English, but they all became silent. That's also the room where I found Clarkie. He was just inside the doorway, sitting down with both legs spread out in front of him, resting upright and leaning back slightly on his rucksack, which had been loaded down with our team's intel gear. Clarkie's trademark smirk was frozen on his face with lips curled in a smile. He looked so peaceful; he had been killed instantly by a round that had come out of my room. I tried to move him from the view of the front door, but he was too heavy.

Clark Schwedler was twenty-seven years old. It would take over a decade for the magnitude of Clark's death to penetrate me. My tears now are often spontaneous, triggered by a fleeting memory, a mixture of accumulated losses, or just a random thought. At that moment, though, I couldn't stop and grieve over Clarkie; I needed to secure the building and protect my teammates.

In another room in the back of the compound, I found the two enemy detainees. Our Iraqi scouts had made entry into this room, discovered the men, and cuffed them. I checked their flex cuffs and then put one of our Iraqi scouts in place to guard them. I positioned our other Iraqi scout on the front entry with specific orders to shoot anyone who tried to come into the house.

I knew that I was shot up. I walked around and cleared the house with my damaged pistol. Each time I turned my head, I could feel my radio earpiece snag on my body armor. However, I failed to notice that my fifteen-pound, suppressed, M4 rifle was still strapped around my body and bouncing between my knees. That's what stress does; it focuses attention and eliminates distractions simultaneously.

I plugged my earbud in and keyed my radio to ask for status in the house, but my radio had been shot—it still had a tone but no signal. My radio was smashed, and I needed to contact the team. I tried to swap out my radio with Clarkie's but my gloves were slippery from all the blood. I had just started to pull off my left-hand glove when I saw that my thumb was barely attached to my hand; it flopped into my palm. There was a bullet hole through the glove—I must have been shot in the thumb when the enemy shot my pistol, destroying my gun's grips. I decided to leave my gloves on. Eventually, I managed to switch out my radio for Clarkie's. I moved back into the room where my gunfight had happened—I felt safer there, as I knew everyone in it was dead. It was there that I made radio contact with the rest of the team. "Hey, this is Mike. I'm still in the house—it's secure. We got four enemy KIA, one Iraqi scout KIA, one SEAL KIA, two detainees, and six women and children."

Jack and the rest of the team had cleared the area and posted up some two hundred yards away from the compound. They had previously considered calling in an air strike to level the compound, but the head count had come up two SEALs and four Iraqi scouts short. Bassam, our interpreter, was one of the missing. He was found terrified, curled up in a ditch, when Jack tripped over him while departing the target. If he had not, Bassam would have just laid there. Fortunately for both of us, no bombs could be dropped because the team could not account for everyone.

April 6, 2007, 1:49 AM

Jack's voice came on the radio. "You okay, Mike?" he asked.

I reported back: "My pelvis hurts and it's hard to breathe. Don't come into the house until you call me, or the guy that I put at the front entry will shoot you."

A minute or so later, I radioed to deconflict the entry so Jack and the team could enter the house. I was sitting with my back against the wall in the room where my gunfight happened, and watched Jack and the rest of my team walk in. I had no idea how badly I was hurt until I saw the looks on their faces. That's the first inkling I had that my wounds were serious. Jack and a few

Me at age 4 in
New Jersey.

Age 18, circa 1990. Head-
shaving party the Saturday
before starting BUD/S. Pink
shorts are courtesy of my
girlfriend and future wife.

First time wearing a dress
uniform with my Navy
SEAL trident.

Circa 1990, SEAL Team 3, Foxtrot Platoon. Training on Piñeros Island, Puerto Rico. I'm on the far left.

Circa 1991, SEAL Team 3, Foxtrot Platoon. Sunset and machine guns on Piñeros. No shower in three weeks.

Circa 1999, SEAL Team 8. Cold Weather Training in Alaska. Hiking up glaciers.

First Iraq deployment, 2005, Green Zone, Saddam's Parade Grounds. L-R: Army Special Forces intel, the Kurdistan president's son, and me.

Iraq, circa 2006. Ordnance and explosives captured on direct-action missions.

Near Fallujah, Iraq, circa 2006–2007. Iraqi Army Scout Training.

Clark Schwedler with his new pet, Master Chief. The dog currently lives with Clark's parents in Michigan.

SEAL Team 4, Foxtrot Platoon. Desert of Hawthorne, Nevada, with 3 Troop. Preparing for my second Iraqi Deployment Unit Level Training.

Second deployment in Iraq, SEAL Team 4, Foxtrot Platoon, circa 2006–2007. Me and Clark Schwedler teaching medical classes.

Iraq, circa 2005. Jocked up, going to work in a war taxi, an H60 Black Hawk helicopter.

Promoted to Navy Chief in Little Creek, Virginia.

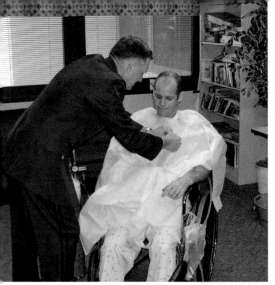

General Brown pinning
on the Purple Heart.

Secretary of the Navy
Ray Mabus awarding the
Navy Cross.

Me and General Petraeus at a
Navy SEAL Foundation fund-
raiser in Chicago.

Hollywood and the half-Ironman, Florida. L-R: Chris Pratt, Me, and Jamie.

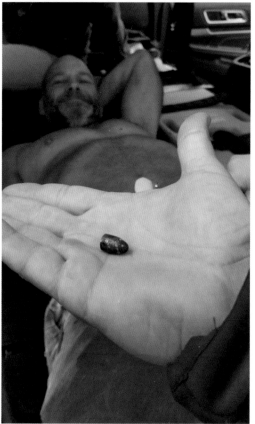

Bullet removal at home, 2019. I had a 9mm round removed from my stomach—from when I was shot during a gunfight in 2007.

of the guys re-cleared the compound. Meanwhile, Doug, Micky, and Jamie helped me take off my body armor. The weight lifted and I felt much lighter. It was still hard to breathe—I thought that the bullet holes in my back may have caused a collapsed lung or pneumothorax-traumatic. One of our SEAL team medics attempted to apply a special bandage to cover the holes, but I was too bloody; the dressing wouldn't stick. I sat in the room with the dead enemy fighters. It was there that Micky and Jamie learned that Clarkie was gone. I could feel their anger, then frustration; their pain would come later and last the longest. Doug let me know the medevac was two minutes out. The guys wanted to help me to my feet, not realizing that I had already been up walking around clearing the house.

"Don't touch me," I said. I was afraid someone would grasp on to one of my bullet holes. "I can walk."

April 6, 2007, 2:14 AM

Fifteen minutes after I'd called the team to let them know that I had been shot, the medevac landed. Jack asked if I needed help as we walked together to the bird, about a hundred fifty yards in all. I felt heavy and slow as we walked together over a freshly plowed field. I put my left arm over his shoulder to steady myself as I moved. Jack instinctively reached up and grabbed my hand, which almost ripped off my dangling thumb. "Jack, let go of my thumb!"

Conner, my SEAL teammate who was wounded in the arm exiting the house, jumped on the bird with me for a short flight to the hospital in Baghdad. He was another one of our team's medics, and I thought that was why he was with me. I didn't know that he had been shot until we were in the hospital together back in Bethesda, Maryland. The flight medic was very efficient, crawling all over me to cut off my clothes and gear and get to my wounds, inserting his knee into every bullet hole in the process. In his defense, there wasn't much of me he could touch that didn't have a bullet hole punched out of it.

When the helicopter touched down in Baghdad, Connor jumped out to help the medical crew on the tarmac. Connor attempted to open a complicated Israeli-made litter with his one good hand, but these litters require a properly trained pair of good hands to open them. It was a real cluster. A few seconds later, a golf cart with a gurney pulled up. At this point, I was totally naked except for my boots—I jumped out of the chopper, slapped Connor on the back as I passed him (our signal that I was the last man), and I boarded the golf cart for a speedy ride from the tarmac to the hospital.

From the moment I was first shot to the moment I arrived at the hospital in Baghdad, forty-five minutes had elapsed—well inside the Golden Hour, the period in which medical treatment of physical trauma has the highest success rate. I had not received any medical treatment up to this point except for the one unsuccessful attempt to patch the bullet holes in my back. The flight medic only had enough time to cut off my clothes and gear before we landed. The medical team at the hospital was excellent—they moved me onto a gurney and rolled me into a hallway flooded with bright overhead lights. The medical staff began rolling me around counting and calling out bullet holes; left leg, right leg, left arm, right arm, buttock, back, left thumb, stomach, shoulder…When they called out the wound to my scrotum, I said, "You guys don't need to worry about that one. I've already had a vasectomy." That's when I passed out.

It appears that the bullet wounds to my upper back and

buttocks occurred when I was knocked unconscious from the grenade blast. I believe that while I was knocked out, one of the enemy fighters stood over me with a 9 mm pistol and shot the two rounds into my buttocks before jamming the pistol under my body armor and firing two into my back, shattering my scapula. I presumed this because I never had my back to the enemy, and none of the holes in my body armor line up with the wounds in my back. Also, we did recover a 9 mm handgun from the room as well—the enemy had stripped this weapon from one of our dead U.S. Army soldiers in a previous attack. The weapon, and other recovered gear, had the dead soldier's name on it. This also may account for the surprised look on the enemy's face when I shot him from a few feet away while on my side. He must have thought that he had already killed me.

While unconscious, I was moved from the hallway of the Baghdad hospital into what would be my first of many surgeries. I awoke the next day on the tarmac in Baghdad, ready to board a C-17 medical transport plane to Germany. I was lying on a gurney sporting an IV and a newly installed colostomy bag. When I lifted my head to peer into the massive cargo hold of the C-17, I saw there were gurneys stacked three high all the way down the fuselage, all full of our wounded—and all of them seemed far worse off than me. I was uncomfortable and embarrassed to think I was getting special treatment.

My SEAL teammate, Chris Tyll, had been assigned as my casualty assistance officer and would accompany me all the way back home. Chris was standing next to me with a satellite phone. "You have to call your wife," he said. I refused at first, but then I remembered that my next of kin must be notified within twenty-four hours of an incident. Brenda was back in Virginia Beach shopping with the girls when she answered.

"Hey," I said, "I don't have a lot of time. I'm coming home early. I got shot, but I'm fine. I've got all my limbs, my face is fine, and the doctors said I'm going to make a 100 percent recovery. I'll see you soon." I handed the phone back to Chris and the medical team stacked me on the plane. I must have passed out, because my next memory is of waking up back in the United States, at the Naval Medical Center in Bethesda, Maryland.

CHAPTER 11

Baghdad to Germany to Home

April 5–6, 2007, Al Anbar Province, Iraq: Chris Tyll, Navy SEAL

I was supposed to be with Mike on the mission that night but had been scratched off the list at the last minute. The operation was to track down the enemy fighters who had recently shot down another of our medevac choppers, killing all onboard. The pilot, twenty-eight-year-old Jen Harris, was a young marine from Massachusetts and a fellow Naval Academy graduate; she'd lived across the hall from me at the Academy. It was her last flight of her third deployment, only days before coming home. Captain Jennifer Harris was killed when the helicopter she was piloting was shot down by the insurgents that we were now going to hunt. There are coincidences in war that defy explanation, and this was one of them: My SEAL team's mission was to capture or kill the people responsible for killing my college classmate. But I would be manning the radio that night back at the tactical operation center, rather than going on the hunt with Mike and the others.

A few hours into the mission, the reports began coming in: troops in contact, standard fare for SEAL missions, but minutes later the reports took on a more urgent tone. "Possible friendly KIAs, enemy KIAs, and multiple friendly WIAs." A medevac was immediately launched to pick up our wounded. A KIA report puts in motion a chain of painful events for loved ones on the other side of the world.

The gravity of the situation soon became clear. We'd lost an Iraqi scout and a fellow SEAL, Clark Schwedler. Clark grew up not far from me in a small town in Michigan, and our extended families knew each other—another coincidence of war. Four insurgents had been shot dead, two were in custody, and six women and children were also secured. We had multiple wounded, including Chief Day. Mike had been shot numerous times, too many to comprehend, but he secured his men before evacuating himself directly from the gunfight to the medevac. After learning of the severity of Mike's wounds and his need for immediate evacuation out of Iraq, I would be assigned to accompany him on his journey to the United States. I would also be the casualty assistance officer for Clark Schwedler.

Mike was flown from the gunfight directly to a Level 1 surgical ward in Baghdad; I arrived shortly after Mike's initial surgery and before he went into his second one. He was full of bullet holes and had tubes running in and out of him. I called his wife, Brenda, who was in Virginia Beach shopping at Harris Teeter's pharmacy. I told her that Mike had been wounded, that he was in surgery, and that I would have him call her when he was out. She was upset and told me, "Don't let him die."

After the second surgery, Mike and I were on the airport tarmac awaiting a flight to Germany. That's when I made another call to his wife and handed Mike the phone. In a very controlled, strong, and "no big deal" tone of voice, he told her what had happened, that he'd be okay, and he'd see her soon. It was impressive; he was totally under control and spoke like he was calling to tell her that he was stuck in traffic and was going to be late for dinner.

After Mike's second surgery in Baghdad, he was still in bad shape but stable enough to transport to Germany for more advanced medical treatment. Mike would be the last patient loaded on the C-17 aeromedical evacuation plane. It was a surreal scene that looked like something out of World War II: the plane was full of patients on Army green canvas litters, stacked high like they were in bunk beds. Medical staff wearing headsets scurried back and forth and up and down. In the rear of the plane, there were two operating rooms with full life support. We were loaded on last, directly into one of the OR ports, with a staff of two flight surgeons and two nurses assigned to us. I strapped in beside Mike. He was out of it, and I held his hand as we took off. Almost as soon as we got in the air, I could hear the other patients' alarms going off. The medical staff was running around attending to different patients all over the plane. About ninety minutes into the flight, Mike turned ash gray and flatlined—the medical team pounced on him and worked frantically to bring him back to life. A couple minutes later, he began breathing and his skin color turned from gray to pink. Then, forty-five minutes later, his skin turned gray and he stopped breathing. The medical team went back to work— controlled, frantic, professional work—and they brought him back to this world. After that second incident, I thought for sure I was going to have to make the call to his wife to tell her Mike hadn't survived the flight. After being revived a second time, Mike woke up and said, "Don't leave. I'm cold. I'm cold." I covered him up with another blanket and kept my hand on his chest. He would flatline and stabilize one more time before we landed in Germany.

News travels fast in the SEAL community. The SEALs who were on the mission had called their friends and recounted what happened once the dust had settled. I'm sure the medical teams who treated Mike in Iraq had relayed the unbelievable number of bullet holes they found in him to their colleagues working in Germany, and then those in Bethesda. Upon our arrival in Germany, nearly every active duty Navy SEAL knew that Mike had been badly wounded and that Clark had been killed.

Mike was rushed from the plane directly into surgery. He would have a total of three more operations in Germany. The medical teams in Baghdad, on the plane, and in Germany were amazing.

Mike was resting after his final surgery when there was a knock on the door. It opened and in walked Admiral William McRaven, a fellow SEAL, and his wife, Georgeann. At that time, he was stationed in Stuttgart, Germany and had driven four hours after he heard the news about Mike. He did not arrive as Admiral McRaven; he came as just another team guy, dressed in a polo shirt and khaki pants. He and Mike knew each other well from their SEAL Team 3 days back in San Diego during the '90s, when McRaven had been Mike's commanding officer. Mike and the future admiral had spent long hours training together. Admiral McRaven asked for details about what had happened and about Mike's condition; he wanted to know about the standard of care. He asked about Clark, and then took inventory on me. I'm sure he saw that I was tired. He suggested that I join his wife for a bite to eat while he shared some time alone with Mike. It had been nearly twenty years since the two had served together, but Admiral McRaven still very much considered Mike a close teammate.

After the surgeries in Germany, Mike was stable enough to fly to Bethesda, where he would undergo yet more surgeries. We boarded another flying hospital and made our way back to the United States. We were again loaded on last so that we would be the first ones off the plane. When we touched down in Maryland, an ambulance with a medical team was standing by to transport Mike to the Naval Medical Center in Bethesda. I could tell Mike felt very awkward—he was accustomed to going first into gunfights, but almost no place else. He was the chief, the senior guy, the leader; his role was to take care of his guys, not have others take care of him. I could sense that being first off the plane and being taken by a waiting ambulance directly to the hospital while other severely wounded patients were waiting—some burned, others missing limbs—made him very uncomfortable. He had the same look on his face that he got right before he tore into someone. I suspect at that moment Chief Day was more uncomfortable with being first off the plane than he was about having a bunch of bullet holes in his body.

I accompanied Mike to the hospital while my wife drove Mike's wife, Brenda, from Virginia Beach to Bethesda to meet us. I took a shower, changed my clothes, and left Mike in the care of the hospital staff and Brenda. I would go retrieve Clark Schwedler and transport him back to his hometown in Michigan, where I would join his family and friends in honoring his life.

The Admiral's Visit, Mike Day

I really don't have any memory of being in the hospital in Landstuhl. Over the years, I've met up with people who say they visited me in Germany, but I don't remember any of them. I was so out of it when Admiral McRaven visited. Twelve years later, he would fill in the blanks for me. He sent me a text that simply said: "Hey Mike—I wrote about you in my upcoming book." Admiral McRaven's first book, *Make Your Bed*, was based on a graduation speech he gave at the University of Texas. The book was an instant *New York Times* bestseller. His text message to me contained a section of his new book, *Sea Stories*, that was all about me. That book, too, would go on to become a bestseller.

Excerpt from Admiral William McRaven's Sea Stories, Pages 262–264

I've learned that life has a mystical aspect to it. As a man of faith, I have felt the hand of God too many times not to know that it exists. But when you see his handiwork up close, when you examine all the possible outcomes and determine that only one outcome is possible—but then something else happens—that's when you know there is more to life than meets the eye.

The nurse at the Landstuhl intensive care unit was almost speechless.

"I've been in nursing over twenty years," she said. "And I've been here at Landstuhl for the past three years. I've seen some of the worst injuries of the war." She started to tear up, but they were happy tears.

"I have never seen anyone shot up this bad." She paused. "He's got sixteen bullet holes in him"—she took a deep breath—"and he is going to be fine."

I smiled and thanked her and her team for everything they had done to save my fellow SEAL. She looked at me, shook her head, and said, "We had nothing to do with it."

I understood. Life is that way sometimes.

The man in the hospital room was Senior Chief Petty Officer Mike Day. Mike had served with me in SEAL Team Three. He was a character: a bit mouthy, in a funny Team-guy sort of way. Always had a joke, nothing seemed too serious, but he was a great SEAL operator and a good sailor. I had lost track of Mike after I left the West Coast. Now we were reunited in the worst of all possible situations. A hospital.

Peering through the window, we could see Mike lying on his back with the usual array of monitors and IVs protruding from his body. The nurse opened the door and cautioned us not to stay too long. Mike still had another surgery to undergo before they moved him back to the States.

As I entered the room, Mike perked up, raised his hand high in the air, and yelled loudly, "Hey, skipper! Great to see you!"

"Michael!" I boomed back at him at an equally high volume. "Are you lying down on the job again?"

"No sir! Just getting ready for the next fight!"

I shook my head and laughed.

As I got closer to Mike's bedside I was stunned by what I saw. There was hardly any part of his body that didn't have a bullet hole. Only his chest, where the Kevlar vest had protected him, was free of wounds.

I sat for about thirty minutes and listened to Mike's story. As the minutes went by, I could see him struggling to stay awake. Finally, he looked me in the eye and said, "Sir, when do you think I can get back to the guys?"

Looking down at Mike's tattered body and the colostomy bag plugged into his bowels, I knew the answer, but sometimes the truth wasn't always the best response.

"As soon as you can kick my ass on the obstacle course, then you can get back to the guys," I said.

Mike rolled his eyes and smiled. "Well, that shouldn't be too hard."

The morphine started to kick in and he slowly drifted off to sleep.

Later that week, Mike was transferred back to the States. His injuries were too severe for him to get back into the fight, but that didn't stop him from serving his fellow warriors. Today Mike helps veterans with post-traumatic stress disorder and traumatic brain injury. He gives back to the nation every chance he can. Over the years that followed, I would run the obstacle course every chance I could, knowing that one day Mike would show up and challenge me. I needed to be ready.

CHAPTER 12

Perfectly Wounded

I had no idea that my next fight would nearly kill me.

My first memory after leaving Iraq was of being awoken by a group of Navy corpsmen carrying me on a stretcher from the airplane into an ambulance. "You guys better not drop me," I said. In the distance, I could hear my wife's voice. I couldn't make out her words, but her Southern accent was like a familiar song playing in the distance; my brain instinctively isolated on its faint sound through all the other commotion. It's funny how our brains automatically catalog, then seek out the familiar to bring us into homeostasis. Brenda's voice was my brain's default comfort programming. She has been part of me since I was nineteen years old, has cared for and loved me for more than half the time I've been on this earth. She knows me better than I know myself. There are well-documented cases of people experiencing physical empathy, or the pain of others. On the night that I was shot, Brenda was out to dinner with our daughters when she said she grabbed the table and doubled over from a sharp pain in her hip. Halfway around the world, at that exact moment, a torrent of bullets slammed into my legs, arms, and pelvis.

It was then that I spoke my first real prayer: "God, please get me home to my girls." He answered it. The Bible describes the union of marriage as "they are no more two, but one flesh" (Mark 10:8). I'm not religious, but I do believe that there is a universal higher power. I don't claim to know who or what that power is, but Mark's description would help to explain Brenda's sudden sympathetic pain: she felt me, and I felt her. We are forever woven together, entangled, mystical parts of each other.

It was in Bethesda Naval Hospital where I learned the full extent of my injuries. My poly-trauma medical team said that I had essentially been "perfectly wounded": I had been shot twenty-seven times, but miraculously all precisely in the right places. Not one of the bullets, or the combination of them all, was enough to kill me. "There is no accurate medical explanation why he survived; by all rights he should be dead," said Mark Russell, MD, trauma specialist and ballistics expert.

Twenty-seven rounds. My ceramic body armor had absorbed eleven of them, three of which were in a tight group into my chest. While they may not have pierced through, the power of the bullets smashing into me broke my ribs, and I had a blood-filled contusion on my right lung. My ceramic body armor was only designed with single-shot protection, which meant that the force of a high-powered round would be absorbed into the brittle plates that would shatter upon impact, dispersing the bullet's energy. My plates did break when the first bullet hit; then they stopped ten more rounds. I don't know how, and neither do the experts.

Another sixteen bullets went into my body. I got shot in both arms, both legs. One round went in my lower right thigh and came out the upper right thigh. I can't explain, and neither can the doctors, how a round traveled up the length of my inner thigh and didn't hit my femur or rupture my femoral artery, but it did. Heck, I'd walked around that Iraqi compound and out to the chopper after the bullet had torn a tunnel through my leg. Days later in the hospital, I could look directly into the top of the exit wound and see light coming from where the bullet entered at the bottom.

I had two rounds in my butt. One went through my intestinal tract, bladder, and rectum. I didn't know for sure if I had been shot in the backside, but my butt was really itching, so I asked a nurse if I had been shot in my behind. She checked my chart and said, "Yes, two times in the butt." I reached under and pulled a plug of bandaging out. Four months later, I located that fully intact 9 mm round inside me when I saw it on an X-ray while preparing to have my bladder stent removed. Nobody knew it was there till that X-ray.

I would have about a foot of intestine removed and would need to wear a colostomy bag for months. Fortunately, only three of the twenty-seven bullets hit bone—the one that nearly took my thumb off and two more that shattered my scapula. Everywhere else the bullets had hit was either soft tissue, or the rounds were stopped when they smashed into my armor plates. I had my right thumb fused at the middle joint. My shattered scapula became a real problem, as it caused such bad swelling in my right arm that the doctors were afraid it would need to be amputated. The medical team pushed my scapula back together under a live X-ray. Fortunately, the swelling subsided and there was not much long-term damage.

Ballistics

To understand what "perfectly wounded" means, it's important to know some basic ballistics and what bullets are designed to accomplish.

Guns transfer the kinetic energy of a bullet into a target. The energy ripples as a shock wave through tissue as the bullet plows through the body, leaving a cavity in its wake. Think of this shock wave like the one a rock makes when dropped into water. The energy delivered into a target increases with the increased mass of the bullet and its increased velocity. Thus, bigger and faster bullets are more deadly because they create a bigger shock wave and transfer more energy into a target.

A bullet's shock wave can create massive internal damage, shattering bones and rupturing organs anyplace in the body, not just in the path of the bullet. My scapula was likely shattered by the two 9 mm rounds that were shot into my back as I lay unconscious from the grenade blast. My three broken ribs and the bruised lining of my lungs were the result of shock wave trauma. Surgeons who treat the type of gunshot wounds that I sustained often report seeing pulverized or disintegrated bones, torn and crimped blood vessels, and liquefied organs. Most of these patients die.

Bullets are not designed to over-penetrate or go straight through a target, because the force that continues to propel the bullet has essentially been wasted and not transferred into the target. This is why some bullets, like most of the ones that hit me, are elongated—so that when they strike, more of their surface area hits the target and does not sail through it. I had been shot a total of twenty-seven times, eleven of the rounds smashed into my body armor, sixteen others entered me. In my case, most of the sixteen bullets that hit my body did not perform as designed or intended. Some of the large-caliber, high-velocity 7.62 × 39 mm AK-47 rounds sailed straight through my body; others were dug out of me in Baghdad. One round tumbled as it exited the enemy's weapon, making it more deadly, but it was stopped when it smashed into my chest plate. This bullet completely flattened on one side when it hit my body armor. Typically, these rounds don't become unstable or tumble until after a hundred or more yards, and this gunfight was within ten feet. My SEAL teammates found this flattened bullet stuck in my vest; they made jewelry out of it and gave it to me as a retirement gift.

One bullet—the 9 mm round that I located in my rear end while lying in my hospital bed—remained lodged in my body for eleven years, and during that time it traveled from my buttocks, around my hip, and came to rest in the adipose tissue of my stomach, aka my beer belly. Long after I retired, one of the guys eventually dug this bullet out of my gut during a dinner break when I was doing a training contract with a group of SEALs. I have a cell phone video of this bullet removal "surgery" being performed in the backseat of an SUV. The round came out of my body in perfect condition; I made more jewelry with it.

Expert Patient Advocate

I was a demanding, unruly patient. The bullet that had grazed my scrotum caused an impressive amount of swelling in that area. Whenever a visitor asked, "Where were you shot?" I'm pretty sure they were asking about the geographic location (i.e., Iraq or Afghanistan), but I was so looped and having fun, so I showed them my personal geography. Brenda knew I was doing it to show off and she would tell me to "quit it." I made her take a picture of them. The swelling has since gone down and they are not that impressive anymore, but at the end of the day, I was happy that particular bullet's path missed the important stuff.

Brenda did not leave my side the entire time I was in the hospital. She was with me 24/7. When she did sleep, it was on chairs and couches in my hospital room. Brenda and some of our friends put a recliner next to my hospital bed. It was a good thing she never left my side, because I was all doped up and yelling at people. The morning after my first night in the hospital, I woke up with an erection and my catheter was still in; the nurse had taped the catheter line to my upper thigh, and my penis was bent in half. I had been shot in both my arms, so I couldn't move them. I was looped on pain meds and yelling at the nurses, "Help, help, look at this. It's way too big. You need to tape that damn thing to my knee." I was half yelling, half laughing, cursing; people were running around; there was confusion and chaos.

That incident set the tone for my hospital stay. I refused to wear my monitors and would pull them off. I was a difficult patient, to say the least. Once, I mistook a volunteer for my urologist and started yelling at him, demanding that he fix my catheter that had become clogged. The kid was part of a program that provides volunteer opportunities for people with special needs. I'm sure that I scared him. I was so stoned that I couldn't distinguish between medical and nonmedical staff. Another time, the batteries for my pain med pump ran out, and the young male nurse was having a hard time opening the battery compartment. I grabbed the pump and tore it out of his hands. "Give me the batteries," I yelled at him. He handed them to me—I tore the compartment open, pulled out the dead batteries, and installed the new ones. I was in a lot of pain, and still a very difficult patient.

I had all sorts of issues while in the hospital, including a serious *Acinetobacter* infection, which is like the Iraqi version of MRSA (methicillin-resistant *Staphylococcus aureus*). It's common in hospitals, where people with open wounds, invasive devices such as catheters, and weakened immune systems spread the bacteria. It's hard to treat and is resistant to many types of antibiotics. An *Acinetobacter* infection starts out as a small, sensitive red spot that quickly spreads and becomes very painful. That infection was far more painful than any of my gunshot wounds. *Acinetobacter* and its cousin MRSA are also highly contagious, and my youngest daughter ended up with a patch of MRSA on her leg.

Brenda was very protective of me. There were visitors she didn't allow to pass through her iron curtain, including Senator John McCain. The senator was visiting the hospital and was to present me with my Purple Heart. I was in the ICU recovering from the emergency surgery to repair my scapula to save my right arm. I was intubated and knocked out. Brenda walked in as they were pulling the intubation tube out and asked what they were doing. They said Senator John McCain was there and wanted to award me my Purple Heart. Brenda replied, "I don't care who is here. You're not going to wake him up. Let him rest." I did not receive it that day.

A few days later, the staff wheeled me out for a photo op with some military brass to present me with a Purple Heart. I had been walking the day before, but now had to use a wheelchair as I wasn't well; my complexion was yellowish, and I felt dizzy. All the brass and medical staff were in the room posing for photos and chatting it up when someone saw that I was really sick. When I couldn't stop the room from spinning, I looked over at General Bryan Douglas Brown, the four-star command of USSOCOM and said, "Dude, you need to hurry up. Something's wrong with me." Brenda knew something was wrong. The party ended abruptly, and the staff rushed me back to my room to check my vitals. My blood pressure had plummeted, and my heart rate was faint and slowing down fast. The doctors hit me with some type of drug, which felt cool as it flowed through my veins, and the room stopped spinning. The medical staff saved me again.

Once I was stabilized, one of the staff happened to look in the trash can beside my bed and saw a few empty cans of Carnation nutrition drinks. I had dropped over fifty pounds since being wounded, and one of my buddies had brought me Carnation nutrition shakes to help fatten me up. I didn't know that the shakes were full of potassium, nor did I know that my IV bag had potassium in it. I had chugged a few shakes shortly before the Purple Heart ceremony, so by the time the event kicked off, I was full-on hyperkalemic. Too much potassium in the blood can result in a fatal cardiac standstill; your heart basically just stops. If I had not been roused for the Purple Heart ceremony, I probably would have died of a heart attack or some type of cardiac condition in my bed without anybody noticing. That episode scared Brenda, and she would guard me closely.

Gary Sinise, the actor who played Lieutenant Dan in *Forrest Gump*, and Mykelti Williamson, who played Bubba Gump, came by to chat one day. Gary Sinise is a huge supporter of our military and veteran community. Brenda liked him, so she allowed him to pass through the curtain. Her intuition while I was in the hospital saved my life, and her persistence would save me again a decade later.

One of the guys who visited was Chaps, a Navy chaplain, who I was always happy to see. Chaps was an awesome guy, funny—a little unconventional for a chaplain, but a perfect fit for the SEAL teams. He smuggled me in tins of Copenhagen dip, and we would chat for hours. He was one of the people who made my hospital stay tolerable, which had nothing to do with the staff; they were all great. I was just a difficult patient. Brenda knew who would sneak me Copenhagen and would catch all of them, except Chaps. I had Chaps sneak it in because I figured she wouldn't check him. I was right—he smuggled tins of dip in a box of tissues.

Checking Boxes

I was told that I would be in the hospital for three, maybe four months. The care was excellent, but I couldn't get any sleep. I wanted to go home and see my girls. After the first week, one of the medical staff would come in every day and ask me the same series of questions and administer the same tasks. I quickly became frustrated and wouldn't answer his questions or do any of the tasks. I saw him writing down my non-responses, checking boxes as he went, and I asked what he was doing. He said, "Recording your answers." Apparently, the tasks and questions were a test, and I was not allowed to leave until I had successfully passed the test and correctly answered all his questions. Correctly checking all the boxes became my mission.

The physical test included walking certain distances unassisted, including up three flights of stairs. One of the tests was a traumatic brain injury (TBI) memory test. I was given a series of colors or words and had to repeat them back in the same order. I already had a terrible memory and could barely remember people's names, but I worked at it. On day sixteen, I finally talked my way into passing the test. I told Brenda to pack up; we were going home. I went to the nurses' station to let them know I was leaving, and the head physician, my primary care manager, or PCM, said, "You're not going anywhere until I release you." My lead doctor was tough and didn't take any of my nonsense. I would try to dictate and control my medical care, and she would push right back and shut me down. She would make me wait hours until coming to see me. When I saw her later that day, I told her that I had passed the test and was going home. "No, you're not," she said. I argued and debated with her for another hour. Brenda had already cleared the room and packed the car with all my gear. I finally wore my doctor down and she signed my release. Sixteen days after I arrived at Bethesda Naval Hospital with sixteen bullet wounds, I was wheeled out of the hospital and walked to my car to go home. I'm sure that the staff was happy too.

My physical and psychological threshold for pain was different due to my life experience, and this incident was more significant to people around me than it was to me. In my mind it just slowed me down some but was really no big deal. At this time in my life, I had little understanding of the dimensions of trauma and that its effects were cumulative. I guess I always compartmentalized my trauma without much thought; it was my superhuman power. If I knew that it was better to address things as they occurred or closer to the event, I would have been better off. I didn't have the capacity or emotional language to understand what was going on inside of me. Thus, trauma accumulated.

La-Z-Boy

Between the bullet wounds and the fresh surgery scars, I couldn't lie flat, so I traded my hospital bed for my living room La-Z-Boy recliner. For the next three months, Brenda would be my doctor, nurse, maid, and cook, while at the same time taking care of our two young daughters. She had to wipe and wash me, unpack and repack my bullet wounds, and dump my colostomy bag. Brenda still refused to leave my side; she slept on the couch beside me and would not fall asleep until I did. She never complained; she just went to work nursing her very difficult patient back to health. I knew that I was healing up when I could lift myself out of the La-Z-Boy and go to the bathroom without waking her. This was a difficult task, and exhausting, but I wanted to do one thing that would give her a break. I made all sorts of grunts, groans, and hydraulic noises pressing myself out of the chair, but as I healed and my strength returned, the grunts and groans tapered off. Brenda handled my medical care, the kids, and everything else like a total pro. She deserves a medal.

My girls were still very young when I was wounded. One day, my youngest daughter—who was six years old at the time—waited until we were alone, then turned to me with a serious look and asked, "Daddy what happened to the bad men who hurt you?" Her question caught me off guard, and it occurred to me in that moment that she was anxious and protective of me. But I didn't want her to know that I had killed people. I hesitated to think of a reasonable answer. "Don't worry, honey," I told her. "I put them all in jail and they are not getting out." It wasn't a full-blown lie; we did hold two of the detainees in custody for a while. Maybe it was my hesitation, but she didn't seem satisfied with my answer. "Okay," she said.

A few weeks later, she brought it up again, looking up at me, her eyes full of determination. "What happens if the bad men get out of jail?"

I stammered, trying to find the right words. "Honey, the bad men are all gone. Daddy killed them. They are all gone."

She listened, let it sink in, and said, "Okay." She seemed relieved and went right back playing like it was no big deal. I had never realized the impact my wounds had on my family. They were mine; how could they bother someone else? My oldest was in high school at this point and her grades suffered. She is now a graphic designer and doing well, but I wish I had recognized the secondhand trauma they were suffering at the time. I only recognized it in hindsight. My trauma had transferred and become theirs too. I wish I had got them the help they needed to comprehend what was happening—to me and to them. I didn't intend to give them a resiliency lesson, but they were strong and managed to find their own personal solace without my help.

I knew that I would never be allowed to operate again, not only because of my being wounded, but also because I was coming up on my retirement. I didn't care—I just wanted to get back with the guys. Four and a half months after the gunfight, I considered myself healed and talked my way back into a new job with the training command as an instructor. I still had a colostomy bag attached to me. I changed it in the men's room at the office. I'm sure I grossed people out, but the guys gave me a pass. In order to get the bag removed, I would need a colonoscopy. I had never had one and so I didn't know what to expect. I did the prep the night before (which was awful). Drink a gallon of poo maker, 8 ounces every ten minutes, then violently poo into my colostomy bag. I changed it, then pooed again. I showed up at the outpatient facility where a nurse with a big beard told me to undress from the bottom down and put on a gown. I did as I was told, then was given an IV and was put on a gurney. The doctor asked me to turn on my side, shot some drugs into my IV, and asked me to count backward from twenty. Instead of counting, I said, "Your nurses are ugly, and this one needs to shave." And then I passed out.

I woke up lying on the gurney in what looked like a gurney parking lot—I didn't see any hospital staff, just a hallway of empty litters. I was alone and had no idea how long I had been out. I thought the staff had forgotten about me. I found my clothes tucked below the gurney, so I got dressed and walked toward the exit. As I was leaving, a person at the front desk asked, "Where do you think you're going?"

"Home, I guess," I replied.

The staff made me wait until the drugs wore off. The doc eventually came out to visit with me and said everything looked fine and my colostomy bag could be removed. Eleven months after being shot, I had one more surgery to reverse the colostomy.

I would spend the next eighteen months training guys, shuffling papers on administrative duty at my new command, and doing long hours of physical therapy to regain what I had lost. My physical therapy team became an important part of my recovery and life. My team was made up of doctors, nurses, physical therapists, chiropractors, and clinicians who specialized in all types of care. Most importantly, this group understood SEAL culture. SEALs tend toward the extreme; we think if one repetition is good, then five hundred must be *great*. I was blinded by my own bias, and it wasn't the first time, or the last.

One day, long into my recovery, I confided to my nurse

that I may have been experiencing symptoms related to PTSD (post-traumatic stress disorder). I had been sitting in my truck listening to a radio talk show, when the expert being interviewed began describing the common symptoms of PTSD. The voice spoke in a calm, matter-of-fact tone, talking about the autonomic nervous system and how sleeplessness, constant irrational fears (which I called "white noise"), and hypervigilance are often normal and predictable responses to trauma. I listened to a stranger's voice describe me to me, and I was both relieved and confused. When I told the nurse, who was a friend and someone I trusted, she smiled and chuckled. "Good to hear, Mike. We all thought that you actually enjoyed what happened to you in that room." She seemed to understand that being profoundly affected by the experience of war was normal, and not being altered was abnormal.

This was the first time that I considered the concept of emotional, "invisible" wounds, and that I had them. I have come to understand that if the experience of war does not profoundly alter you in some way, then you may actually have a problem.

When the doctor said that I had been "perfectly wounded," it seemed like a metaphor for my life: I had been beat up just enough to not kill me, and through the process, I earned the perfect scars of wisdom I needed to survive my next thrashing.

I still had no idea how the events of my childhood influenced my thoughts and behavior. I had become very good at compartmentalization. My self-awareness grew as I uncovered the layers of trauma. I later found that my childhood wounds had prepared me for a career in the SEAL teams, but they also became my most haunting ones. Ironically, it took being shot twenty-seven times to uncover my original wounds, ones that I never considered or knew I had.

Part III

AWAKE

Lulled in the countless chambers of the brain, our thoughts are linked by many a hidden chain; awake but one, and in, what myriads rise!

—Alexander Pope

CHAPTER 13

The Enemy Within

I fully accepted all the hazards of my chosen occupation. Being wounded was no big deal to me. At no time during or after I was shot did I ever think that I was going to die. I was provided the best medical care available and was sure that my physical wounds would eventually heal.

The real battle began when I returned home. The war in Iraq was straightforward—I was expertly trained and had the unconditional support of a community of like-minded, highly motivated professionals. As a SEAL, I had been institutionalized, in a sense: I knew the culture, the people, the rules, and the objective. After leaving the military and returning home, my life became a confusing, frustrating, and stressful mess. I was a prisoner who had been released from the institution into a strange new world. There was a distrustful cynic slowly working his way inside me. His voice sounded like my own, and each day he became more convincing. I was surrounded, isolated, and desperate. This enemy knew all my weaknesses; he was relentless, and he eventually overpowered me. The enemy was me.

CHAPTER 14

Case Fixer vs. Case Manager

In March of 2010, a month before my official retirement from the Navy, I accepted a case manager position with the Special Operations Command Warrior Care Program, better known as the USSOCOM Care Coalition. It was almost exactly three years to the day since I had been wounded.

I went from being James Bond 007, a tip of the spear, top-of-the-food-chain operator, to a social worker. I didn't know it at the time, but this role, the people, my boss, and the efforts I was engaged in would end up being the most important work that I have done thus far in my life. I was humbled, educated, and inspired by what I experienced and the people who I had the honor to serve. I honestly believe I was a far better social worker than I ever was a SEAL.

The USSOCOM Care Coalition is a powerful organization. It's an advocacy group staffed by many former Special Forces operators who are tasked to care for their warrior brothers and sisters. When one of our own becomes wounded, ill, or injured, the Care Coalition is notified, and a warrior advocate like me is assigned to the service member as a case manager. SOCOM contracted these advocacy services from 9Line LLC, a veteran-owned small business and the brainchild of my boss, Scott Heintz, a former Army medevac pilot. The company name is significant to warriors: nine-line means "rescue." When things go bad, someone calls for a medevac using the standard nine-line request. We are all trained on how to calmly provide the nine pieces of critical information required to ensure that a medevac crew gets to their injured parties as fast as possible and with everything they need to save lives. These lines are:

Line 1. Location of the pick-up site.

Line 2. Radio frequency, call sign, and suffix.

Line 3. Number of patients by precedence

    A—Urgent

    B—Urgent Surgical

    C—Priority

    D—Routine

    E—Convenience

Line 4. Special equipment required

    A—None

    B—Hoist

    C—Extraction equipment

    D—Ventilator

Line 5. Number of patients

    A—Litter

    B—Ambulatory

Line 6. Security at pick-up site

    N—No enemy troops in area

    P—Possible enemy troops in area (approach with caution)

    E—Enemy troops in area (approach with caution)

    X—Enemy troops in area (armed escort required)

Line 7. Method of marking pick-up site

    A—Panels

    B—Pyrotechnic signal

    C—Smoke signal

    D—None

    E—Other

Line 8. Patient nationality and status

    A—US Military

    B—US Civilian

    C—Non-US Military

    D—Non-US Civilian

    E—EPW

Line 9. NBC Contamination

    N—Nuclear

    B—Biological

    C—Chemical

Medevac choppers are not armed, and their patients include service members, civilians, allies, and enemy wounded. They race into the unknown to save lives. For those of us who have been wounded, comfort has a very specific sound, and it's the thumping sound of medevac chopper blades. After I was shot, one of my SEAL teammates calmly called in a medevac and provided the nine lines of critical information to the flight crew. My medevac crew arrived at 2:14 a.m., racing into a hostile location just fifteen minutes after the nine-line call. The enemy fighters who I killed had shot down four of our defenseless medevac helicopters; none of the helicopters, crew, or their patients survived. Every warfighter on the ground takes special care of our medevac guardian angels. Care Coalition case managers adopted this same mentality, rushing into the chaos to care for our wounded brothers and sisters.

To understand what makes the Care Coalition powerful, it's important to understand the relationship between Trauma and Agency. Trauma steals. It takes away; it robs us. Trauma can cause the loss of one ability, or many. Trauma can also delete emotions or our capacity to experience a full range of them. Worst of all, trauma isolates; it separates us from the ones who love us, the One who made us, and, most importantly, the love that we should feel for ourselves. Over time, trauma can morph people into victims and render us feeling powerless. Trauma acts like a virus, infiltrating our bodies and minds, hijacking our language. I would hear people refer to their traumatic experiences as "my PTSD" or "my injury." These phrases are the echoes of trauma.

Traumatic events are what happen to us. If I decide to take possession of the traumatic experience in my thoughts and language, then the trauma will eventually become part of me, like a limb. Once transmitted, the virus waits until it's triggered, usually by stress. When enough stress builds up, untreated trauma collaborates with other factors to take over our thoughts and behaviors. This is why trauma is so dangerous—the damage caused by the subsequent behavior causes far more harm than the original wound. I have done my best to make peace with my past and understand how trauma has affected me. I keep my demons close, so I know when they are influencing my behaviors. I give them the appropriate level of attention because they are a part of me, and I have to live with them.

If you have not experienced some type of trauma in your life, then stand by, because you likely will. Trauma comes in many forms and impacts people differently. The type of trauma doesn't really matter; losing a limb, losing your job, the death of a loved one, a cancer diagnosis, a brain injury—all of these events steal something from us. The point is trauma is trauma—losing your job and therefore the means to support your family can be just as traumatic as being shot twenty-seven times. Both involve the loss of something, and the struggle to recover after the fact. One of the peculiar characteristics of trauma is that it connects us. We are attracted to the familiarity of each other's trauma. It's peculiar because the same familiarity that attracts us causes conflicts that separate and isolate us.

Childhood trauma profoundly shapes us, and left untreated, I think it's the most destructive kind, because the perpetrators are supposed to protect us.

Agency, in the psychological context, is your ability to act, influence, and control your destiny and your life. If trauma is about loss, agency is about gaining, taking back, and empowering. My new role at the Care Coalition was to join with my warrior brothers and sisters as they fought to gain back what they had suddenly lost. The Care Coalition is powerful because it creates a sense of agency. It's powerful because when two fully committed people stand and fight together, the odds change—we become our own force multiplier.

My clients became my new swim buddies, and I never, ever, leave my swim buddy. Together we confronted a bureaucratic health care system filled with delays and often irrational decisions. We would confront the losses head-on and claw back lost ground every day. My clients all had different needs; many had family histories like my own, and they were warriors like me. I'm sure that many of them experienced trauma as children, or as the study called it, *adverse childhood experience.* Trauma attracts others affected by trauma, because we are comfortable with the familiar. Our subconscious minds, maybe even our souls, know each other long before we ever meet.

Looking back over my life, I can see how trauma robbed me and how I responded to gain back a sense of agency over my life. I endured years of beatings at the hands of my father and felt powerless until I mustered up the courage to smash him in the chest with a bat. After I did it, I felt more in control of my life, even powerful. I felt the same thing after the two-by-four-crowning incident during my time at Job Corps, and after I dumped my stepmother on her backside when she attempted to slap me. I responded in the only way I knew at the time—I confronted violence with greater violence. I like to say that I never started a fight, but the truth is, I never really tried to avoid them. Fighting gave me a sense of agency. Confronting the commander during boot camp about my orders and timing my own runs in BUD/S boosted my confidence and purged my fears. I mustered up the courage, confronted the loss, and took control of the situation and my life. I also felt a sense of agency when I graduated from boot camp, BUD/S, and jump school. In that small room back in Iraq, alone, outnumbered, outgunned, and being shot while lying on the floor, fighting back was the one thing I knew how to do. Fighting to get up after being wounded, fighting to get out of the hospital, gave me focus. When I'm stuck, I get up and keep fighting. It gives me a sense of agency. I also believe this may be why I enjoyed meeting with the high school kids after my Leap Frog jumps. I had no idea what the concept of "agency" was back then, but I believe that sharing my personal story with those kids empowered them, and me.

I now see that I tend to want control over lots of other situations. Clarkie, Jamie, and Micky would often tell me, "Chief, stay out of our back pockets." They wanted me to trust them and let them do their jobs. The need for control and agency is a defense mechanism against loss and has, at times, made me an overbearing person.

My new job at the Care Coalition gave me a sense of empowerment too. I had been in the Navy all my life, and the thought of ending my career and losing my income was concerning to me, to say the least. The Care Coalition provided me agency over my future, and it allowed me to help do the same for others. I was not yet fully healed from my own wounds, and my new role allowed me to investigate a wide variety of treatment options for myself and others.

There is a complex matrix of government, private, and non-profit organizations that provide health care and transitional services to wounded service members. My approach to it was much the same as when I was deployed: I took ownership of the role, found a phone list, and started making calls to learn who owned the "battle space." I basically did the same thing that I did when I arrived on the job in Iraq. I figured out what exact information each agency needed to gain benefit approvals; then I submitted it on behalf of my clients. Eleven months after I started the job, I attended my first case manager training. It turned out that I had learned more through my own self-directed training than many of the other case managers. The class instructor and other case managers were even asking me for suggestions. I'm a big advocate of charging forward and learning by doing. I have a SEAL Team 8 challenge coin that reads *Fortune Favors the Bold*. And it's true.

Navigating this Rubik's Cube of care can be overwhelming and often discouraging. My Care Coalition clients were engaged in daily physical and emotional battles—they didn't need to be fighting to gain access to the care they were promised or other services on top of everything else. My job was to learn what type of assistance they needed and make it happen. I would investigate all manner of treatment modalities and programs.

Most of these organizations were unknown to each other, and none of them shared information or coordinated care. One of the biggest challenges was that these organizations didn't understand how we do things in the SEAL teams. We are not accustomed to excuses, unreasonable delays, or the word *no*. SEALs like to fight, and we like to win; this is how I was trained. I went into my new social worker job not as a "case manager" but as a "case fixer." My clients were going to win. I would measure my worth by the amount of benefits that I was able to secure for each one of my clients. When a request for care was denied, I took it personally and would work to get it reversed by any means necessary. I can proudly say that this attitude almost got me kicked out of one VA hospital, and I think I may be on the less-than-welcome list at several others.

Simply put, the people I worked for and represented deserved the best of care. I found no reason to be polite to hospital staff or case managers that I felt were providing insufficient care. One day, my boss got a call from a case manager who said, "I don't appreciate your guy coming into my office like a bull in a china shop and telling me how to do my job." As I told my boss, someone had to let her know that she wasn't doing "her job." It was all worth it for the people whom I was privileged to represent. Their wounds were so much worse than mine. They are the greatest examples of human resiliency that I have ever encountered. They motivated and humbled me; I was honored to be their care manager.

One particular hospital staffer stands out in my mind. She was the case manager for one of my clients, a Marine Special Operations Command or MARSOC Marine who was wounded during a ten-hour firefight in Afghanistan. He took a sniper's round to the head that went through his helmet and penetrated three inches into his brain. The entry was high on his forehead and it exited out the back. It was a terrible, penetrating wound. This case manager was doing nothing for his continuation of care until my verbal foot kicked her right in the ego. The images of my client's skull—or lack thereof—were unsettling. When I saw his skull replica, an entire side was missing. How could anyone survive that? If being shot in the head was not bad enough, the wound had caused him to stroke out, resulting in him losing function to his right side.

When I asked him what happened, he said they had heard shots from the opposite valley. He was on an Mk 47 automatic grenade launcher and sent a few rounds downrange. Just then an enemy bullet smashed through the glass and hit him in the frontal lobe. He got up and ran to the medevac helicopter. "I fell asleep thinking I'm going to wake up in Afghanistan shaken up but with a little speech therapy I'll be back in action. I woke up in Bethesda, and I knew it was serious." He would have to relearn how to talk, walk, almost everything. He was stoic about it, and never asked me for anything. I would go visit him and hang around for a few days to learn what he needed; he was one of my favorite people to spend time with. He was always good-natured and never asked for anything. He has since recovered, earned his bachelor's degree, and secured a job tracking down human traffickers and child pornographers using computer forensics.

Mark was one of my SEAL brothers, an old-school Navy chief. When I arrived at the Care Coalition, Mark had been living with ALS (amyotrophic lateral sclerosis) for years. He was still strong as a bull, though, and fearless. But his condition had worsened to the point where he could only slightly move his head, and he needed a new wheelchair. I sent a request to the VA, and they denied him. I was pissed. This was not about a chair—this was about my friend's dignity; he was my SEAL brother and I was not going to let the VA do him like that. I hauled ass over to the provider, walked into their office, and closed the door. Mark and I were going to win; I was certain of it. I also knew that it was going to get ugly, but I didn't care. My buddy Mark was going to get his chair, and his dignity. Several weeks before he passed from this world, he got his chair.

Hope Trauma

Holly was one of my first clients. When I met her, she was only able to lie in bed and scream at the top of her lungs—it was scary. Holly was raised in Port Angeles, Washington, and enlisted in the Navy after high school. She'd joined the military to create a future for herself and her family. When I met her, she was still the breadwinner for most of her family. She had become an Independent Duty Corpsman, which is the highest enlisted medical care provider in the Navy. She had graduated the program and become an Arabic linguist. Hospital Corpsman Chief Petty Officer Holly Crabtree was assigned to work with a SEAL team as they conducted various operations in Iraq. It was April 15, 2010. I had just joined the Care Coalition, and Holly was nearing the end of her deployment. She was out doing a medical civilian affairs operation when she was shot. A bullet pierced her helmet, fractured her skull, and settled behind her eye. She was not expected to live. Her crew realized that she was "expectant" and coded Holly's condition as "Hope Trauma." She proved everybody wrong. Holly would not give up or stop working. She would have to relearn how to talk, walk, even swallow. I watched her do it all—it was both sad and humbling, but most of all, it made me very proud to know her. Holly has since made an impressive recovery and is medically retired after thirteen years of service.

"I Felt the Heat"

"As soon as I stepped on it, I knew I had lost my legs." In May 2012, Navy EOD2 Tech Taylor Morris, a young, all-American kid from the Midwest, was leading a team in Afghanistan when he stepped on an IED. "As I somersaulted through the air, I watched my legs fly off. I was still conscious and bleeding out, and I told the medics to stay away—I didn't know if there were any other bombs, and I didn't want anyone else to get hurt." Taylor lost both legs and both arms in the explosion.

Taylor became one of my clients soon after I started. His family and his girlfriend, Danielle, were by his side night and day. Taylor never once complained; he just took it one minute at a time. He quickly relearned how to walk on prosthetics. Danielle was great; before Taylor got his new legs, he would wrap his stumps around Danielle's neck and hips, and she would carry him like a rucksack. Once Taylor got his legs, he never looked back.

Hunting Trips

On Veterans Day weekend in November 2011, I was invited by the Navy SEAL Foundation on a hunting trip with a few other SEALs to a private ranch in Texas. Private, high-fence hunting ranches are big in Texas, in both ways; popular and vast. It's a great concept. The animals are very well cared for, the grounds are pristine, and the hunts are mostly successful and well organized. It's like a wildlife farm. I really enjoy hunting, but for me it's more about the experience than the meat.

The SEAL Foundation had also invited a group of their friends and major donors. We hunted quail, which you need about fifty of to make an appetizer; others were hunting deer. One of my hunting companions for the weekend was political consultant Karl Rove. We chatted about politics, strategy, hunting, fishing. I told him how I got wounded. We had some great conversations. He shared his background, and I learned that he was no stranger to loss and trauma. I would later find out that his mom had died by suicide. These days, I feel that it's safe to assume that everyone has been affected by some degree of trauma and that our behaviors have been influenced by these events. By that measure, judging others is unkind at best, hypocritical at worst.

Not long after the hunt, Karl wrote an op-ed piece in the *Wall Street Journal* about our meeting and the trip.* A few years after that, I gave Karl a call to ask if he could help one of my SEAL buddies who was running for office. My former teammate was campaigning in a Maine state election as a Republican. Maine Republicans are like mopeds—rare and unpopular. The campaign was a steep uphill battle, perfect for a SEAL, and I figured Mr. Rove could offer my buddy some tips. He ended up losing the election, but he still loves Maine.

A year or so later, another nonprofit organization sent myself and Dan Cnossen, one of my SEAL brothers and my

---

* Karl Rove, "Hunting with SEALs," *Wall Street Journal*, November 17, 2011, https://www.wsj.com/articles/SB10001424052970203611404577042073983018102.

Care Coalition client, on a hunting trip to Namibia, Africa. We would be joined by actor Tim Abell, a former Army Ranger who at the time was the host of a TV show on the Outdoor Channel. I don't know how to describe Dan Cnossen, other than as a powerful force of nature. Dan graduated from the Naval Academy in 2002, cruised through BUD/S, then did a combat deployment in Iraq before deploying again to Afghanistan. "I was in advance of the rest of my platoon—this was at night in southern Afghanistan, at a pretty remote location— and I stepped on an IED. The blast was quite severe; I was in a coma for about eight days and I woke up at a naval hospital in Bethesda, and I can't get out of a wheelchair. I have a ruptured bladder, colostomy bag, broken hands, shattered pelvis with an external fixator, two legs amputated above the knee...at that point it was pretty much ground zero." I would witness Dan go from learning how to walk again to finishing the New York City Marathon in 2:38:00—26.2 miles in two hours and thirty-eight minutes. He used the marathon as training for the 2014 Paralympic Winter Games in Sochi.

When we arrived in Africa, Dan settled into his hotel room and immediately put on his legs and went for a run. He ran every day we were there. I felt guilty after a few days about him running alone, worried he might get eaten out there, so I joined him. Dan, Tim, and I spent two weeks in Namibia walking around, stalking animals, and hunting. The Namibians were in awe of Dan; his muscled arms were thicker than most of their bodies. They had no idea what to think of his prosthetic legs.

Dan has gone on to compete in two Paralympic games so far, Sochi in 2014 and PyeongChang in 2018. He's won a total of six medals: one gold, four silver, one bronze. If that's not impressive enough, in his spare time he earned a master's in public administration and another master's in theological studies from Harvard. I recently watched a video of Dan surfing for the first time, and he's already crushing it.

I share the stories of my Marine buddy Mark and Holly, Taylor, and Dan to prove that there are so many other veterans I know who have been wounded far worse than I was and recovered. They have found ways to keep going and live what I feel are "Powerful Lives."

CHAPTER 15

Climbing Mountains

The peak of Mount Rainier reaches 14,411 feet. It's the most glacially covered mountain in the lower forty-eight states and the tallest in the state of Washington. It's a massive mound that dominates the western Washington skyline; you can't miss it when you fly into Seattle.

Outdoor physical activities connect my mind to my body like nothing else. Surfing is my favorite activity, but I really enjoy anything that gets me outdoors. I believe the mind–body connection can have powerful healing effects. I would take my Care Coalition clients on outdoor adventures at every opportunity. There is nothing like a hard physical challenge, a good kick in the butt, to make you feel alive. In July of 2010, I joined a group to climb Mount Rainier. Our climb team included my friend and fellow Navy SEAL Jason Redman. A month after I was wounded, Jason took machine-gun rounds to the face and arm when he and his team went after an element of the same terrorist cell that shot me. Two other SEALs on the climb team were Brian Smith, who had survived an IED blast that had sent shrapnel through his brain, and Kevin, a Navy medic who was wounded when the Humvee he was riding in was hit with an IED.

Other members of the climb team included Scott Parazynski, a Harvard-trained medical doctor and former NASA astronaut. Scott is an avid mountaineer and reached the summit of Mount Everest several years prior to our climb. There was also Walt Leonard, a dentist from South Carolina and a huge supporter of service members and veterans; Wynn Tyner, a retired Marriott executive; and Robert Vera, a successful entrepreneur and bestselling author. The climb was sponsored by Camp Patriot, a veteran-focused nonprofit organization.

Climbing Mount Rainier is serious stuff; on average, only 50 percent of the able-bodied climbers reach the summit, and every year an average of three people die in the attempt. We were mostly able-bodied, but it really didn't matter—we were climbing it anyway. I needed these types of adventures, and I knew the other guys were excited for the climb.

We all met at Sea-Tac airport and together made the trip to Ashford, Washington, to gear up and go over the plan. Curtis Fawley and Art Rausch would be our guides. The pair had guided on the mountain during their college years and together had over three hundred round trips to the summit. They had both gone on to pursue other careers, but came out of retirement to lead our group. Curtis's fourteen-year-old son, Keegan, was also with our group, along with several local guides to help carry extra food and gear.

We spent the first night at Whittaker's Bunkhouse, owned by the Whittaker family, who are climbing legends. The place was jammed with other climbers—seems like everyone who climbs Rainier passes through Whittaker Mountaineering on their way to the hill. The next morning, we all piled in the van for a ride up to Henry M. Jackson Visitor Center located in an area called Paradise. This is where we would start our climb.

Paradise sits at six thousand feet above sea level. I have spent most of my life *at* sea level, or slightly below it while surfing or diving. Maybe that's why I felt my lungs burning while walking around the parking lot...

Curtis knew that most of us were low-landers and some of us came with bullet holes, so he demonstrated the "rest step" method of walking. Basically, it's step, rest, step, rest. Very slow and methodical, but my lungs and legs appreciated the technique. We'd start the hike at six thousand feet, and rest/step our way up another four thousand vertical feet to Camp Muir. It would be at ten thousand feet from Muir that we would launch our summit bid. Muir is basically the base camp for all the climb teams trekking to the summit by way of the Disappointment Cleaver route. This is the fastest and most direct route to the top. I had not put a pack on since being shot, and I had some crazy muscle spasms even before we started walking uphill. The hike up to Muir put the hurt on me, but I couldn't let anyone know. When we arrived, I unpacked, helped to organize the tents, hydrated, ate dinner with the team, and crammed into my tent with Jason and Brian on a slice of frozen mountain away from the other groups of climbers.

Rainier is covered in snow and ice year-round, and even summer storms can roll in and dump snow. I woke up the next morning cold and stiff, but good to go for a summit bid. We would spend the day learning how to use our ice axes to self-arrest and avoid falling into a deep crack in the ice or pitching off the mountain in the event of a fall. After the lesson, we rested most of the afternoon and had an early dinner of chili, beans, and mac and cheese. As soon as the mountain was cold and hard, we would attach crampons to our boots, rope together, and move in rope teams toward the summit.

Late in the afternoon, the winds picked up and the day turned dark. The weather forecast indicated a summer storm rolling in off the Pacific. Rain below six thousand feet and snow above it with sustained winds of forty miles per hour and gusts of seventy-plus miles per hour. A seventy-mile-per-hour wind gust would be more than enough to chuck me off my feet and toss me to the bottom of the mountain. We would not be climbing up or down for a while. I piled into my tent with Jason and Brian to wait and listen. The weather delay was unexpected; if we had known it was coming, we would have taken the chili and beans off the menu. There are consequences to these foods, and I swear that being in altitude and being crammed together in a small tent amplifies them. That night and all the next day, the winds pounded us, sounding like an angry freight train—we could hear the gusts winding up and then a blast would slam into our tent and bend it in half. There were a few times that I thought for sure we would be blown off the mountain.

We got a break in the weather and Curtis and Art gave the thumbs-up. We would make a run at the summit that night as soon as the snow turned back to ice. Crampons, the metal spikes attached to the bottom of climbing boots, don't work well in slush or soft snow. It was about 10:00 p.m. when Curtis knocked on our tent and said, "Saddle up, boys. Time to climb a mountain."

We all noticed that Jason was not looking or sounding well. He was coughing up neon-green chunks and looked exhausted. Doctor Scott checked him out and made a preliminary diagnosis of bronchitis or some other type of respiratory infection. Jason had been shot in the face—the round entering the back of his head just behind his ear and exiting out his nose—and another machine-gun bullet had hit him in the elbow and almost took off his arm. Any other person would have been dead. An infection was not going to hold him back. He told Doc Scott, "Thanks, I'm good."

We launched out of Camp Muir at 11:30 p.m. and headed toward our first major obstacle: Disappointment Cleaver, a rocky outcropping that separates two glaciers. Two hours later, we arrived at the base of the cleaver. A year or so earlier, my buddy Brian survived a penetrating brain wound after being hit with shrapnel and had to relearn how to swallow, talk, and then walk. Now the guy was trudging up a big mountain. The cleaver is steep, like climbing a ladder, and at the time it was mostly exposed rock with some areas of hard-packed snow. I could see sparks above me generated by the other climbers' metal crampons grinding against the rocks. The route is extremely narrow, basically a one-way trail. There was a group of sketchy climbers above us, moving very slow and kicking rocks down at us. Then *ping, clank, clank, ping, clank, ping*, and someone above me yelled, "Look out below!" A climber in the sketchy group above ours had lost his grip on his aluminum ice axe and it was bouncing down the rocks, headed straight for us. You don't want to be in the path of an ice axe; they're all business and no fun, with sharp points at each end. Luckily, nobody was hit.

It took us about an hour after that to navigate up the cleaver; then we took a rest break on the steep glacier a few hundred yards above it. I was already smoked, and we had hours more of uphill climbing before we would reach the top. Jason sat with his head down; he didn't talk. We ate, drank, then rallied and moved up the mountain, walking around a series of huge crevasses. The moon was so bright I turned off my headlamp. Looking out to the east, I could see the lights of Yakima, Washington, some seventy miles away. We would take one last rest break, then do a steady push all the way to the summit. Five hours had ticked away since we left Camp Muir, and now the sun was coming up and the summit was in view. Brian was chugging along, and Jason moved forward with his head down like he was on autopilot; he was hurting but would not quit or complain. I was crushed hours ago but kept moving. One last push and my rope team stepped into the summit crater. Mount Rainier is a volcano, and you can smell sulfur and feel steam welling up from deep inside the earth. It releases through cracks all around the top. We celebrated and took photos; Jason took a nap. One of the photos was of Scott, who'd brought the same American flag he'd taken into space and to the summit of Mount Everest. We gathered around it and snapped a picture with it on the summit of Mount Rainier. A few hundred yards across the crater, there was a small rock outcropping where a guest book is stored in an ammo can. The last thing I wanted to do was more walking, but I figured that I may not get back this way again, so I made the trek and signed the book.

The way down seemed more dangerous than the way up because in the daylight we could actually see the steep incline and how far down the landing would be if we fell. The sun created another hazard, melting the rock-hard snow into slush and rendering our crampons useless. Most of my way down was a controlled—or out of control—slide.

Our climb had been in honor of Ryan Job, another Navy SEAL who had been wounded in Iraq by a sniper, an injury that had left him totally blind. I had only met Ryan once, at Mike Monsoor's Medal of Honor ceremony at the White House. (In September 2006, Navy SEAL Mike Monsoor was on a rooftop in Ramadi, Iraq, fighting it out with some insurgents when a grenade landed beside him. He could have just jumped down the hatch to get out, but instead he jumped on the grenade. He died thirty minutes later; his teammates were wounded but all survived.) In 2008, Ryan Job climbed to the summit of Mount Rainier blind. A year later, in 2009, he died as a result of a hospital error. Most people know Ryan from the books *American Sniper* and *A Warrior's Faith*. He was the character Biggles in the film *American Sniper*. On my own way down, I closed my eyes once and gained a new, profound respect for Ryan Job—I couldn't take ten steps without opening my eyes.

One common characteristic that I have seen among SEALs is an ability to effectively manage fear. As SEALs, we do so much scary stuff that we need to deconstruct and control fear. The most common fear is the fear of the unfamiliar or the unknown. SEALs have been conditioned to override this natural fear response. We have learned that the odds of success are far better if we boldly move forward into the unknown. What makes SEAL training different is that we are taught to handle both known and potential threats. A "potential threat" is one that we may have never encountered before and is basically unknown. SEALs are trained to step forward into the unknown and handle whatever we encounter. I don't believe that all SEALs are fearless; it's just that they feel fear and do it anyway.

We moved down from the summit in a slow-motion slide. We landed back at Camp Muir in the early afternoon. The extra food that the other guides carried up for us would be our lunch. Eventually we all made it down the mountain without any missteps. When we arrived at the bottom, Jason needed a round of antibiotics to kill the bloom of bronchitis growing in his lungs.

Climbing mountains forces you to build trusted relationships because you are all tied together with ropes. If someone slips and falls, it's up to everyone else to save that person. There are deep crevasses all over the mountain that swallow people. I learned that a member of the Whittaker family is buried in one of those cracks on Rainier. If you survive the fall and manage not to drag your rope team into the crack with you, then the only way out is by the other members of your team working together to haul you out.

Climbing Mount Rainier came at the perfect time in my recovery. It empowered me and gave me a sense of agency after being wounded. The climb also connected me with all the right people, many of whom I have built trusted relationships with. Over the years, I have brought more of my Care Coalition clients on adventures with the nonprofit group Camp Patriot. Jason Redman and Brian Smith are still close friends. A year or so after the climb, Walt Leonard hosted a white-water rafting trip for me and some of my Care Coalition clients. Whenever I visit Arizona, Wynn Tyner rolls out the red carpet for me at the Marriott Camelback Inn. Curtis Fawley helped Brian find work as a mountain guide after Brian retired from the teams. Robert Vera has become a close friend and is the coauthor of this book. Each of these trusted relationships, along with the new skills I've developed, has become a critical part of my personal resiliency portfolio.

CHAPTER 16

Breakthrough and Breakdown

June 2014

As a case manager at the Care Coalition, I would investigate all types of treatment programs for PTSD, TBI, and other common issues experienced by my clients. Many of the programs were considered alternative to conventional medicine or hybrid programs that combined conventional and Eastern medicine. Representatives from different treatment programs would attend our Care Coalition meetings and share information about their work. I consider myself an open-minded person and have met all sorts of people claiming to have a fix or an effective treatment for PTSD or TBI. "Open-minded" is my polite way of saying that I'm extremely skeptical, but I'll try your voodoo to see if it works. I felt that it was my job to test any treatment program that I was going to recommend. I was the crash-test dummy for all manner of programs, and I did find some symptom relief in acupuncture, chiropractic care, and working with several clinically trained behavioral health therapists.

One of these Care Coalition presentations was on how

meditation can help calm the mind and be an effective sleep aid. I wasn't sleeping, and I guess it showed, because my fellow Care Coalition case managers pointed at me and said to the presenter, "If you can calm him down, we'll believe you." After the presentation, I was invited to participate in the program. I accepted on the basis that I would evaluate it for my clients.

This was a weird time in my life. I felt overwhelmed at work. On top of this, I had recently become aware of long-suppressed feelings of childhood shame and guilt that were really bothering me. At times, my stress level was beyond anything that I had ever experienced in the SEAL teams, and apparently it was showing enough that even my coworkers could tell I wasn't sleeping. Work became a never-ending onslaught of problems, and my clients trusted and relied on me; they were depending on me to get the medical treatment they wanted and the income they needed to pay all their bills. There was one crisis after another, urgent calls coming in at all hours of the day and night.

Meanwhile, my living situation was in transition—we'd sold the home that we had owned for fifteen years and purchased a five-acre lot outside of town. We were building a new, larger home. I had been happy in our old home, and I wasn't 100 percent all in on the new house, but decided to roll with it. All four of us were crammed inside a hot, double-wide trailer in the Virginia summer until the new home was built. My commute time to the office doubled, with thirty stoplights on my new twenty-six-mile route. The building costs were constantly escalating, and there were all sorts of delays. I was the sole source of income; I was totally responsible for the mortgage, three car payments, food, two kids, my wife, and everything else. Apparently, moving, buying a home, money issues, and problems at work are some of life's most stressful events. I had all four happening simultaneously.

Two weeks after hearing the guy talk about meditation and sleep, I decided to go check out the program. I drove from Virginia Beach to the treatment facility four hours away. I arrived late that night and had to make a call to find someone to check me in.

I was assigned to a log cabin with a few other guys. I was the last person to arrive and would be sharing a room with another participant. I walked into a room in the cabin—the door was wide open, the light was on, and there was already a person asleep in the lower bunk. I thought he must have fallen asleep with the light on, so I shut it off and he immediately jumped up and freaked out. Apparently, he needed to sleep with the lights on.

I found a place to sleep, woke early the next morning, and went for an easy run. The entire place had a weird energy to it. I threw up after my run, which had never happened to me before after such a light run.

One of the first group exercises was journaling about our individual traumas to understand their origins. I enjoyed this exercise because it allowed me to examine the wreckage of my childhood in an objective and constructive way. The exercise was to identify what had hurt you. I used my father. I had to describe what he had done to me and how he made me feel. I described the helplessness, terror, and fear he caused. I then had to describe good things I learned from him. I was taught to be strong-willed, given the ability to act under extreme duress, and not to be harmful to others. I then thanked him for the good he gave me and honored him.

In another session we watched a video on the ascended

masters: Jesus, Buddha, and a few other well-known spiritual leaders. We also had daily classes on meditation.

On one of the breaks I overheard a counselor and a participant having a serious conversation about astral projection. I was an open-minded skeptic coming in, but I nearly packed up and took off after listening to them go on about transporting themselves to different places.

On Thursday, after doing multiple days of different types of meditation, including transcendental meditation, things got very weird. I was having new thoughts, and vestiges of my past would suddenly well up in my consciousness. I was not meditating at the time and was just sitting in a room with the group when my attention was drawn to a chair across from me that looked like it was made from driftwood or some other type of unique wood. I watched as the legs of the chair slowly transformed from wood into human bones and skulls right before my eyes. I was wide awake, talking to people while watching the chair literally morph into bones.

Then I had an intense déjà vu experience. One of the guys, who I'd first encountered snoring in the lower bunk, seemed to take on the persona of my father. I had the sense that somehow my father had invaded this other guy's body. It was like he became my father's avatar. He had the same personality as my father, a know-it-all, loud bully, just like my father. I was trying to remain calm, but I felt like I was losing my mind and was paranoid and freaking out inside, trying to keep contained.

We were all going to do an equine therapy session and there were two beautiful horses in a corral. I had this eerie sensation that my wife's persona was present with me and that the two beautiful horses somehow represented my daughters. At that moment I felt an overwhelming urge to protect them all. While the other participants went into the pen with the instructor, I stood outside the corral. When I turned and looked at an instructor's face, it was like some type of Hollywood special effects scene. I was staring at him and his damn face morphed into an evil demon. I froze, terrified and trembling. It felt like every cell in my body was vibrating violently. I just stood there and closed my eyes and prayed, "God, please help me, please God, please." I was sure these people were going to hurt me. When I opened my eyes, everyone was gone. I needed to get out of there. I saw the group standing in the corral and said as calmly as I could, "Hey, guys, thanks for everything. This has been really good, but I need to leave, like, right now." The instructors tried to talk me out of leaving, saying that it wasn't safe for me to go, and I stood there thinking, *Well it's definitely not safe for me to stay here with the demon dude.* I tried to hide it, but I think one of the instructors may have known that I was freaked out. One of the female instructors gave me a ride back to my cabin—I made her use the GPS, so I knew where she was taking me. When I arrived back at the cabin, I grabbed my bag, chucked it in my truck, and immediately started driving back to Virginia Beach.

That's when things got really strange. I had a four-hour drive back home, and all the while I was trying to figure out what in the world had just happened to me. I calmed myself down and planned to drive the speed limit all the way home, when I'm usually a ten-miles-per-hour-over-the-posted-limit kind of guy. I was on the road for no more than thirty minutes when I saw a car veer off the highway and smash into the butt-end of a guardrail and come to a stop about a hundred yards into the grass median. Nobody was stopping. I pulled over to help. The car's airbags had deployed; the driver, an older guy, was dazed. He was alone and claimed that he had been cut off. I told him that I had watched him drive off the road and that nobody had cut him off. He said he had stopped to get a bite to eat down the road. I asked if he was a diabetic and he said yes. "I think you had a blackout from diabetic shock," I said. I stayed at the scene and rendered medical aid until several police officers and a tow truck arrived. I then sat with the cops and gave them a full accident report. I'm thinking to myself, *I can't be crazy. I'm providing medical care. I'm here with the police providing a witness statement to an accident that I just saw. Did what I see back at that treatment facility really happen?*

The accident was a two-hour ordeal. When I got back on the road, I called some friends on the drive home to describe what happened and to make sure that I was not totally nuts. I called my nurse friend who treated me after I was shot and asked her to meet me at a hospital in Virginia Beach. I needed to have my blood drawn and get a dangerous drug panel—I thought for sure that I had been drugged. I was so disturbed by the experience and paranoid, I thought that people had conspired to harm me. I met my friend at a Virginia Beach hospital emergency room and said to the intake nurse, "I need a dangerous drug panel." Of course she asks, "Why?"

What was I going to say? *Well you see, the reason I need a drug panel is because this afternoon I saw a dude's face morph into a demon, and this was right after I saw the four legs of a chair turn into human bones.* I didn't answer her and instead asked, "How much is it?"

She said, "Twenty-five dollars."

"Great, here's my twenty-five dollars. Let's do it."

The drug panel came back negative. I was totally clean, nothing. I really wanted the panel to show some kind of drug, chemical, anything. That would have been the easiest explanation for what I had experienced. I was fully expecting it to come back positive, which would have meant they may have also been dosing the other participants. I was paranoid and terrified. Whatever that experience was, it changed my life. I arrived home and attempted to explain to my wife what had happened. I was so scared that I scared her. She was furious at the treatment facility and demanded that I never go back there.

My intent in going there was to evaluate the place to learn if their program could help people get more sleep, but instead the experience terrified me so bad that I slept even less. When I did lie down to rest, I was so paranoid that I kept my pistol under my pillow.

For years I have attempted to re-create the experience, but nothing has come of it, not even close. After lots of late-night Googling, I have concluded that what happened to me was either a Kundalini Awakening, a spiritual crisis, or a psychotic break. It's possible that these are all one and the same, depending on one's perspective. In the years since, I have read about and met people who have claimed to have had similar experiences. These people come from all walks of life. That event changed my life more so than any other that I have experienced before or after, including being shot twenty-seven times. Apparently, my experience is common but not widely discussed, probably because it's scary and people will think you're crazy. A university study found that as many as 25 percent of people who meditate have a bad trip. I would count mine as an exceptionally bad trip.

One study found the following: "Scientists conducted a questionnaire study on 1,232 people for two months. The participants were asked to meditate a couple of times weekly and share their experiences. Although the scientists were expecting positive feedback, the participants explained their experience as worrisome, terrifying, and disturbing. Some of the participants said meditation resulted in distorted emotions and thoughts and changed their perception of the world."*

Nearly all who experience a Kundalini Awakening report the feeling of intense vibrations that last for a few seconds to hours. During this awakening period, the images that are revealed can either be good or evil. There are many reports of suicide after having a Kundalini Awakening.

I had no idea what a Kundalini Awakening was until I Googled "vivid colors, violent cell vibration, demons." *Merriam-Webster* describes Kundalini as "the yogic life force that is held to lie coiled at the base of the spine until it is aroused and sent to the head to trigger enlightenment."†

I'm fully aware of the risks associated with this disclosure. Some may write me off as mentally ill; however, during the entire time, I was able to objectively evaluate the way I was thinking. I knew full well that what I was seeing and experiencing was unusual. I also knew that I was paranoid. I was totally rocked and terrified but could clearly separate my rational, objective thoughts from the unusual experience that I was having. At the hospital, I knew if I told the intake nurse why I wanted the dangerous drug panel, she would have thought I was nuts. I was objectively evaluating my own crazy experience. I was skeptical of the program before going into the place, knowing next to nothing about meditation or mantras. I did

---

* Marco Schlosser, et al., "Unpleasant Meditation-Related in Regular Meditators: Prevalence, Predictors, and Conceptual Considerations," *PLoS ONE* 14, no. 5: e0216643, https://journals.plos.org/plosone/article?id=10.1371/journal .pone.0216643.

† Lawrence Edwards, Ph.D., *Awakening Kundalini: The Path to Radical Freedom* (Boulder: Sounds True, Inc., 2013).

know that telling anyone who I did not fully trust about the experience would make me appear paranoid and crazy. I believe that mental illness is the inability to objectively and rationally evaluate your thoughts and actions. I could do this, but I was still terrified.

I did tell Scott, my boss, what had happened. He listened carefully and asked if I was okay. "I don't think you should go back there," he said. This is what made Scott one of the best leaders I have ever had the pleasure of serving with. I trusted him. He cared about all of us; he *was* one of us. In the SEAL teams, rank doesn't really matter all that much; reputation and trust have currency and authority. Scott had both—a great reputation, and I trusted him.

CHAPTER 17

Ironmans and Hollywood

I didn't allow the bad meditation trip to deter me from finding new, innovative treatments for my clients, and myself. There was a Texas-based nonprofit organization delivering treatment programs for TBI and PTSD. I knew a SEAL, Elliott Miller, who had gone through their program and had excellent results. Elliott is an amazing guy—sharp, witty, and determined. He had been badly wounded, lost his leg, and had been wheelchair bound. He was able to walk after several weeks into the program. I was beginning to think that TBI and PTSD could be related, and if the brain injury could be resolved, then maybe the symptoms of PTSD might also go away—or at least lessen. I decided to check it out myself and go through their two-week program. I just could not in good faith recommend a program to any of my clients unless I'd tested the product for myself. The last test did not go that well, with the demons and all, but I figured nothing could be worse than that.

I traveled from Virginia to Irving, Texas, and met with a patient advocate who had a passion for helping veterans. The clinical program was run by an integrated group of medical professionals that included chiropractors, medical doctors, and a few other specialists. I spent the first week doing a series of assessments and tests. One of the first tests I was given was a pharmacogenomic test that analyzed how my unique DNA would affect my response to different drugs. Drug-gene testing—or pharmacogenetics—is relatively new. The genes we inherited from our parents determine our height, eye color, blood type, and all sorts of other traits. There are also specific genes that are responsible for how we react to medications. Pharmacogenomic tests look for changes in genes that may determine whether a medication could be an effective treatment or cause serious side effects. The test itself was simple and painless—all the doctor had to do was swab my cheek with a big Q-tip and get a saliva sample.

By this point, it had been eight years since I was wounded. I had been given dozens of medications, and I never once had heard of a pharmacogenomic test. I thought it was a great idea. Individual DNA is used in all sorts of ways, and it's now normal to test the DNA of people participating in new drug clinical trials. Law enforcement and the court system both use DNA evidence to include or exclude individuals as suspects. It seemed like it should be a regular medical test, but it wasn't, at least not back then. Nowadays, home DNA test kits from 23andMe, AncestryDNA, and other companies have become hugely popular.

When my DNA test results came back, the clinician asked me to sit with him in his office. He closed the door and pulled out my test results. The results revealed that I should never take any antidepressant medications or any drugs that are in the SSRI (selective serotonin reuptake inhibitor) family, which ruled out Prozac, Paxil, Pexeva, Zoloft, Celexa, Lexapro, and Viibryd. I hadn't taken any, but I had a lot of clients and friends who were taking them. The test identified that if I did take them, then I could have an adverse reaction.

SSRIs are the most commonly prescribed antidepressants. The FDA requires that all antidepressants carry black box warning labels, the strictest warnings for prescriptions. In some cases, people may have an increase in suicidal thoughts or behavior when taking antidepressants. Apparently, this pharmacogenomic test was able to sort out that based on my DNA, SSRIs could cause the worst of all the side effects: suicidal thoughts. I later looked up "pharmacogenomic tests" and found places like the Mayo Clinic and other leading medical organizations all do these tests and highly recommend that others do the same. I was kind of shocked. I thought of my father, who'd been on all kinds of drugs, and nobody had ever tested him. I also thought about the suicide epidemic happening across our nation and around the world. The United States alone has lost more veterans to suicide than we have in the wars in Iraq and Afghanistan combined. My fellow warriors are taking their own lives at a rate of twenty-two each day, on average. How many of my warrior brothers and sisters could have benefited from this $150 test?

In my experience, medicine is not an exact science, and I really liked the way this organization went about investigating individual patients to learn as much as possible before prescribing a treatment program. Most medical treatment programs are designed for the masses; they tend to be reactive and diagnose symptoms without concern for the underlying causes. I am not a "group" and I don't reside within the "bell curve of the norm." I am an anomaly, but then again, we all are. Health care treatment should be specific to the individual, and that cannot be done without proper analysis of the individual. The staff spent a full week working with me to learn how I tick. That kind of care and attention was invaluable.

The second week was devoted to developing and refining a specific program to treat the insomnia and memory-recall symptoms I was experiencing. One part of my treatment was to sit in an "off-vertical axis rotation device," something like a flight simulator that spun around like a gyroscope. I sat focused on a single spot while being twisted and rotated around. Later, a special diet was recommended, and I used other equipment to improve balance and memory. I am not sure if it was the program or the people, but it was the first time in years that I was able to sleep through the night. The doubter in me thought the whole thing could just be a placebo effect; then it occurred to me that that meant I was the placebo, and if that was true, then I could control my symptoms and get some sleep. Whatever the case, I liked the way they did things and was interested in helping them raise funds so that they could treat more people.

I returned to Virginia and eventually settled on an idea to raise funds while competing in a half-Ironman triathlon. I had never done a triathlon, but I had done a few cycling events. I had made it through BUD/S, I was a decent swimmer, and I could run. The distances seemed reasonable: a 1.2-mile swim, a 56-mile bike ride, and then a 13.1-mile run. I had about six months to train—easy. Work was really wearing on me, and looking back now, I think training for the triathlon was a way for me to avoid having to deal with all the demands of my job.

I didn't really have a specific dollar amount that I wanted to raise; I just wanted to help. Robert Vera helped me create a CrowdRise fund-raising page and then drafted a press release, which he sent to exactly one media outlet: CBN, near my home in Virginia Beach. A few days after he sent it, I got a call from

CBN saying they wanted to come out and do an interview. Mark Martin, a journalist from CBN, came to visit me and produced a great story. He explained that I had been shot twenty-seven times, showed my damaged body armor, and said that I wanted to give back to others by raising funds for brain injury treatment by doing a half-Ironman triathlon. The story aired on CBN news and then posted on social media.

Someone at Fox News saw the story and called me. A week or so after the CBN story, I did a live interview with Tucker Carlson from Fox News. I was more nervous doing the live interview than being in a gunfight, but the interview seemed to inspire people. My CrowdRise campaign page grew from about $20,000 in donations to over $100,000 in a few days. Donors who saw my story on CBN and Fox visited my CrowdRise page and made generous donations and left sincere comments. Some donated in memory of their loved ones who had struggled with PTSD; others donated in the name of those who they lost in the war or the long battle that followed. I knew how they all felt. Their loved ones were just like me and many of my Care Coalition clients. I was really humbled by their comments. Former President Bill Clinton donated $10,000 and he sent me a coin that I gave to my father-in-law. My friend sent the CBN and Fox social media links to the folks who run Ironman, and they sent a photographer and reporter. I was the cover story on the spring 2015 edition of *USA Triathlon* magazine.

Jamie, my former SEAL teammate who was with me when I was wounded, had since gotten out of the Navy and was working with Hollywood film star Chris Pratt. I had no idea who Chris Pratt was, since I don't watch much television and don't care to follow pop culture and I had not been taking in many movies recently. But Jamie and I had kept in touch, and I told him what I was doing. He had already completed a full Ironman triathlon a few years before in Louisville, Kentucky, without even training. Jamie is good-looking, smart, and ripped; he looks like a male model and is one of the few true gentlemen I have ever met. Both my daughters think he's cute; heck, everyone thinks Jamie is cute. About two weeks before my half-Ironman race, Jamie called me and said that he and Chris Pratt would like to join me for the race. I thought that the extra publicity couldn't hurt if Chris Pratt would advertise the effort. My friend who generated all the media got me set up with a hotel near both the race location and Disney World. My wife and daughters joined me for a few days of rest and Magic Kingdom rides before the race.

Race Day

I was relieved for race day; I had trained for months with my friend Marci Gray, a great triathlete and a USA Triathlon–certified coach. She is also a total hammer; I couldn't keep up with her and was grateful when race day came because it meant that I didn't have to chase her anymore. All the training and diet stuff was wearing on me, and I was finding it impossible to focus on doing my day job at the Care Coalition. I felt tired, sick, and worn out most of the time.

I met up with Jamie and Chris Pratt the night before the race. Chris was a lot bigger than I thought. We chatted for a while, exchanged some war stories, then came up with a simple race-day plan. We would all start the race together, then do our best to swim 1.2 miles, bike 56 miles, and then run 13.1 miles. We would look for each other on the run and attempt to all cross the finish line together.

There were about fifteen hundred racers in the water ready for a staggered start. When the gun sounded, it was a chaos of arms and legs; it looked like a massive fistfight. I swam on the outside and managed to get out of the water without getting too beat up. The bike segment was hot and muggy, but that's Florida, which is like a humidor mixed with hurricanes, mosquitoes, and alligators. I made it to the run and found Chris and Jamie. We shuffled along in a slow run/walk rhythm with lots of fluid and fuel stops. Our plan worked out, and we all crossed the finish line together.

In the end, I raised over $135,000 for the nonprofit brain treatment facility in Texas and helped fund two of my Care Coalition clients who later visited the facility before the for-profit division of the treatment center filed for bankruptcy and the group closed its doors. I'm not sure if Chris Pratt's presence helped me raise any more money, but it was fun doing the race with him and Jamie. His involvement did help raise the need for a different approach to treating our veterans, which was the main goal. The folks at Ironman were so impressed with the effort that they offered me a spot to race at the Ironman World Championships in Kona, Hawaii, that October. I was over-whelmed and honored—it was like a gift and punishment all in one. The half-Ironman had been a real kick in the butt, and the thought of doing a full one was intimidating. I said yes anyway. I took two weeks off, then started training all over again.

I was totally exhausted and burned out before the half-Ironman; now I was training for double the distance. After the race, word spread about what I was doing, and new donors came to my CrowdRise page to support me doing the full Ironman. But I was at the point where I just could not do my job anymore; I was totally burned out, and the Ironman fund-raising and training did nothing but add to my stress. Everything started to escalate in my mind; I could feel something was on the verge of breaking. The stress of work, training, and financial obligations was all becoming too much. I couldn't sleep, becoming edgy and difficult to get along with on the best of days. Forty-five days before the Kona race, I emailed the Ironman folks to thank them for the opportunity and backed out of the race. I contacted every donor and offered to return all their money. I was a mess.

At work, I would get urgent calls from shrinks who would say stuff like, "Come get your guy." Some of my clients would scare the medical staff, and the doctors knew if they called the police, all hell would break loose, so they called me instead. I would have to go and defuse the situation. These "evolutions" were exhausting, and looking back, they were well beyond my area of expertise.

I would do the minimum reporting at work, then try to sleep or play video games in an attempt to distract myself from the constant fear of something bad happening. I was trapped without an escape route. Stress accumulates, and it was all piling up inside of me. I had no financial help, and I'm not one to ask for any. I was sure that I was going to get fired from my job. This was only the second real job I'd ever had in my life other than being in the Navy. Men are providers; it's instinctual. We like to hunt, fish, grow food, build shelters. The thought of losing it— of not being able to provide for my family or help my clients— was swelling in my mind, and it was damaging what I believe to be my innate identity and sense of purpose. I felt embarrassed and ashamed and emasculated. I would not leave my home for days on end. I avoided talking to people, even turned off my phone. Brenda was troubled—she knows me so well. She was gentle at first, asking me if I wanted to talk to someone. As I became more isolated and combative, she reached out to my friends and coworkers. They joined with her, and together they all hounded me to get help. In a year, I'd gone from training to do an Ironman triathlon to not being able to get off my couch. I was in a dark, dangerous place.

CHAPTER 18

The Right Relationships

If you could only sense how important you are to the lives of those you meet; how important you can be to the people you may never even dream of. There is something of yourself that you leave at every meeting with another person.

—Fred Rogers, creator of
Mister Rogers' Neighborhood

My life had become unbearable. There was guilt, but I think the real culprit was shame. Guilt and shame are very different and controlled my thoughts and behaviors in distinct ways. Guilt was about what I had done, or, in my case, what I hadn't done. Shame was about who I was, or at least who I thought I was. I felt like a prisoner being brainwashed every day. My mind seemed to be stuck on a one-track narrative that became darker with each episode. Every minute of every day, there was this weird repeating internal monologue that opened with guilt, which created a feeling of shame. I would fixate on things that supported this monologue like bailing out on the Ironman, which I was sure disappointed the donors, the treatment facility, my clients, and my family. My anemic efforts at work reinforced my shame. That's when all the "what ifs" began chiming in. *What if I get fired from my job? Will we lose the new house and all my money? What if the people who donated to my fund-raiser think I'm a fraud because I didn't do the full Ironman?* These thoughts would lead to embarrassment, which deepened my feelings of shame. I was trapped in this desperate repeating irrational monologue that all sounded rational to me. I personally knew people like Dan, Mark, Holly, and Tyler, who all had far worse injuries than me—and far more stressful lives—and who were all managing themselves well, but for some reason I just couldn't put things in perspective. I was locked in an irrational, disproportionate, escalating mental prison.

I sat in my truck. I had researched how to do it, exactly where to place the barrel and how to angle the gun. I had practiced it with a cleared weapon and pulled the trigger. I didn't want to leave a mess for someone else to clean up. I would not do it in my truck, so someone else could use it. The bullet would go through my heart; there would be an instant of pain, and then I would be gone. I would do to myself with one bullet what four enemy fighters failed to accomplish with twenty-seven. I stared at the black gun in my hand. I had used one like it to kill before. I was numb and sad, confused and tired. I had cried alone so many times.

My downward spiral had come to its final resting place, and at the bottom was hopelessness. The built-up stress, the lingering effects of trauma, and my physiological deficits all colluded to create a condition of hopelessness. My mind worked trying to come up with an explanation to justify my final act to my two beautiful daughters. Years ago, in that room at the compound, the thought of not being able to see their faces again terrified me. Images flashed in my mind—holding my daughter's little hand in my own as we sat together. The way the girls would wrap their arms around my neck and hug me. Their soft little voices called out me: "Ohhh, Dad!" Their smiling faces flashed repeatedly in my mind.

There was the disproportionate feeling of guilt and shame that relentlessly stalked me. I still felt trapped in a life layered with overwhelming stress, endless responsibilities, meaningless tasks, and toxic people, of whom I felt I was the most toxic. It was all my fault. I felt I was my own worst enemy. This time there was a bullet in the chamber. I was beyond contemplation; my mind was made up. I mentally paced back and forth, working up the courage, the same way I had when I hit my father with the bat. I was getting out of my truck when my phone rang. I looked down at the number. It was Scott Heintz, my boss. I picked up my phone in one hand and held my gun in the other. I let it ring again, not wanting to answer. I couldn't do it with Scott calling, so I put down my gun. I answered: "Hey, Scott, what's up?"

"Mike, I want you to take the next three months to chill out. I'm going to pay you. Relax, take your time, and find a new job. I'll help you however I can. You're beyond burned out. You did amazing work. There is a time limit for how long you can do this job, and you maxed it out." My boss and good friend had just given me the hope I needed to climb out of the very deep hole I had found myself in. In that instant, I would not have answered my phone for anyone other than Scott. Scott had seen it all before. He knew that I was surrounded by wounded, sick, and injured people all day. Scott also knew that many of the people who I'd been meeting with every day for years, including patients, their family members, veterans, service members, and hospital staff, were struggling with depression. "It's like an alcoholic tending bar—you can only hold out for so long. If you are around depressed people all the time, you'll become depressed too."

I suspect that some of you reading this may now think that I'm crazy and write me off. Thank you for coming this far with me. For the rest of you who have ever been depressed or suicidal, I can tell you that while I fully believed at the time that I was thinking rationally, I know now that I was not. My irrational thoughts had started repeating themselves: the world will be better off without me. I don't care anymore, I just want out of here. I'm a horrible person. My future will just be filled with more of the same stress.

These thoughts all seemed totally rational and true in my compromised state, but I had no clue that my thinking was compromised.

What scared me the most about these thoughts and the entire experience is what happened to me just a few months later. Brenda, in her desperation to help, convinced me to visit a physician who had a protocol to treat depression and other conditions. I resisted at first, of course, but finally agreed to work with the guy if only to get Brenda—and everyone else—off my back. It was either this new doctor or I was headed for an inpatient treatment facility.

Gut Feelings

I had been a skeptical participant in every treatment program I'd ever visited. I was an unruly patient during my time at Bethesda Naval Hospital; I did things my way in the hospital and while recovering at home. I was already suicidal without drugs and I wasn't interested in taking any medications based on what I saw at the Care Coalition and what the other doctor had told me after my DNA test. I would check the boxes again with this new guy to get everyone off my back. I was in a low, nasty place and had no real interest in following anyone's magic treatment program.

My first visit with Dr. Anthony G. Beck, the new guy, was over Skype. I gave short answers to all his questions. He ended the call by saying that my test kit would come in a few days. The kit arrived on schedule and was simple enough. I provided samples of everything, including saliva, urine, stool, and blood. (I'll admit, collecting three of my own stool samples, then packaging them up and sending them in the mail was a little weird.) A week or so later, I had another Skype call with Dr. Beck to review my test results. He believed that I was dealing with a serious bout of depression brought on by a number of physical and environmental factors.

Understanding the Modern Operating Environment

Dr. Beck explained how he viewed the world and his methods and philosophy. He described the modern world we live in like an asymmetrical war. There are insurgents lurking everywhere—in the food we eat, the water we drink, and the air we breathe. Blue light emitted from LED lights on our computer and phone screen can cause sleeplessness. The nonstop barrage of Wi-Fi and cellular and radio emissions interfere with our brain waves and can trigger memory issues and other

health problems. These insurgents infiltrate our bodies and dis-
rupt every system and process. "Most people have become totally desensitized to our environment, especially the foods we
eat, and the daily medications taken to manage the diseases created by the foods we eat. It's an insidious cycle. When you add
genetics, trauma, and stress to all this, our bodies, brains, and
minds can become completely altered. Why do you think there
has been a sharp increase in illnesses like depression and diabetes over the past few decades?"

I knew what he was saying about human nature was true.
In Iraq I'd seen people become quickly desensitized to sounds
of barking dogs, helicopters flying overhead, and gunfire, all of
which could have been hazardous, if not lethal, to their health.
At home, I saw people practically washing down their diabetes
meds with sugary sodas. Their soda consumption was likely the
main reason why they had diabetes in the first place.

There was a time when I would rate restaurants by how
much food I got for the price. I started to think differently about
it. Now I consider food as a kind of drug, and Dr. Beck's education reinforced this idea. He put the onus on me by telling me
that I was in control of my health and well-being, and that I was
the only one who could get myself back into a normal, healthy
condition. I liked this—it was almost as if the guy already knew
I was an unruly patient who wanted control, so he gave it to me.

Dr. Beck emphasized that my biochemical makeup and
unique genetics set me apart from every other human being on
the planet, and that I needed to be treated differently than everyone else. The DNA test I did at the Texas treatment facility the
year before had confirmed this. Beck's words rang true to me
because they reinforced things that I already felt. I think this is
how I know the truth—I feel it in my gut. Unknowingly, I had

been on a decade-long search-and-rescue mission to find a way to not only regain what I had lost to trauma, but also to understand who I really was and what I wanted in my life. Every doctor and treatment facility that I had visited over the years added a different piece to the puzzle. Even the bad experiences turned out to be good ones as they clearly showed me what didn't work.

Objective Feedback Loop: The Test Results

I'm a practical guy and need to see objective evidence, not listen to guesses or theories and be convinced of things, especially when they're about me. The blood, urine, saliva, and stool tests were objective, and they definitely came from me. My results weren't good, though: he said that the major issues were that I was lacking some essential "gut flora" and that my hormones were completely out of whack. I learned that what I thought was "me" was *not* me. That voice in my head, the desperate monologue that sounded like me was not me. The real me had been kidnapped by billions of insurgents. We are all a combination of our own human cells and trillions of other microorganisms. Our own human cells are outnumbered by at least ten to one by foreign invaders, microorganisms living in us. All our foreign microbes are unique to each of us—we pick them up from places we visit, foods we eat, and other people. We can't live without these foreign microbes; some help to break down foods we eat into nutrients that are absorbed as beneficial compounds, like vitamins and anti-inflammatory substances that can't be produced by our own human cells. What I didn't know was that gut microbiota irregularities can directly induce depression and can influence our behavior and thoughts by way of a connection called the *microbiota–gut–brain axis.* My gut flora was out of whack from a combination of a poor diet, stress, and all the antibiotics I took before and after being wounded. Dr. Beck said that this imbalance had a name: microbiota–gut–brain axis dysfunction.

I had been working for nearly six years with dozens of different doctors, investigating all manner of treatment programs for depression, PTSD, and anxiety, and I never came across a link between gut bacteria and brain function. Then again, I never had my stool tested either. Dr. Beck said depression is inseparable from brain neurotransmitter imbalance and that research showed that gut flora influences this imbalance. This was back in 2015, and as of this writing, the microbiota–gut–brain axis has been linked to Parkinson's disease and several other conditions. Dr. Beck said that the idea that abnormal gut flora is at the root of mental disorders, including depression and anxiety, was not new. The idea had been around since 1908, when it earned the Nobel Prize for Physiology.

The Underlying Causes

Based on my test results, Dr. Beck believed that my depression was induced slowly over the years, as by the snowballing effect of stress, poor diet, genetics, antibiotics, and chronic inflammation. He said that while it's true that my genes might predispose me to depression and that other stressful events like adverse childhood experiences (ACE) can trigger depression, the ever-increasing incidents of worldwide depression deviates way too far from statistical estimates. Major depressive disorder is now one of the leading causes of disability, morbidity, and mortality worldwide; one in five people probably suffers from it at some point in their life. Dr. Beck explained that we now know major depression is not just a mental disorder, but is also a physiological disease, and that gut microbiota probably plays a crucial part in the onset of depression. Most people, including me at the time, believed that depression was purely a mental disorder. Unfortunately, there are also some who still believe that depression and PTSD are indications of mental weakness. I have experienced both and have withstood some of the most ruthless physical, mental, and emotional conditions without breaking. These long-held beliefs, that depression is solely a mental disorder or one reserved for the emotionally weak, are both totally false. They have created a deeply entrenched stigma around the condition, a stigma that I am determined to erase.

I was stunned. I didn't really know what a neurotransmitter was or did, but I did know many of my fellow veterans and others were struggling like I was. Many of these people were either self-medicating or were on all types of meds, desperate for relief. Some had reached hopelessness like I had and lost the fight to the voice in their head. I'm in no way whatsoever suggesting that anyone should stop taking any of their medications. As it turns out, some antidepressants do actually inhibit the proliferation of certain gut bacteria. However, I am strongly suggesting that people investigate the physiological factors that may be contributing to their conditions, be it depression, PTSD, or any other neurological or brain-related disorder. I suggest finding a holistic doctor to help guide you.

Treatment Plan

Dr. Beck's explanation and my treatment plan included bits and pieces of things that I had heard from other doctors and the new concept of gut health. He prescribed a regiment of probiotics, hormone therapy, and exercise. He said it was important that I continued to get off the couch and move. Even walking would be enough. I also needed to chill out and change my eating habits, eliminating certain types of foods and adding others. He said that there may be several other contributing factors, such as exposure to radio waves like Wi-Fi, Bluetooth, and blue light from computer and phone screens. I was playing video games for hours on a sixty-inch screen. I realized that I only played video games when I was depressed. These factors were likely messing up my brain function. He recommended that I shut down my home Wi-Fi at night and avoid blue light.

I had my mission.

CHAPTER 19

New Thoughts, New Job, New Life

It took about two months, and even then, I only followed Dr. Beck's treatment program about 80 percent of the time. Brenda managed my entire dietary regimen. She would shop for all the foods, meticulously prepare and measure all my meals, and keep a detailed food log. She never stopped being my expert patient advocate and loving caregiver.

I'm sure that the process was gradual, but one day, I woke up and felt like the black cloud that had been hovering over me for years was gone. I was able to function, to move, and to think clearly. The fog had lifted, and the constant, negative internal monologue inside my head had stopped. I felt strong, clear, and confident enough to get up and start moving forward.

I grabbed my phone, opened up my contact list, and started sending text messages and making calls. I needed a new job. Working a phone list and calling people is what I had done when I arrived in Iraq and when I started at the Care Coalition. I needed to get unstuck and move forward, and this was the only way I knew how. A couple months after I started reaching out to my contacts, I got a message from a defense contractor who I had sent a résumé to a year or so before. It's been my experience that as soon as you're fully committed, the universe conspires to help you reach your goals. I hadn't even contacted them; they reached out to me with a position in Virginia Beach as an Air Operations Trainer. Some twenty years after jumping out of planes with the Leap Frogs, I would put these skills back to work as a contracted instructor for Naval Special Warfare, Group 2 TRADET Air Cell. I would train the next generation of Navy SEALs how to jump out of the sky and return safely to earth.

It was great to be back with the boys. I was surrounded by can-do people who motivated and pushed me. It was basically like being in the SEAL teams again. We would do some of our training in Virginia, then travel out to southern Arizona to do jumps over the desert. Arizona is one of the main training areas for military flight and skydive training. It has over three hundred days per year of clear skies, and lots of wide-open air space and terrain. We would jump at night and spend the days working out. I took Dr. Beck up on his advice and found some places to hike and explore. The Sonoran Desert is green and lush and hardly resembles a desert at all. I did a hike just outside of Tucson to a series of waterfalls that looked more like Hawaii than the desert. One weekend, I drove out to Sedona down a two-lane highway when the road made a bend to reveal massive red rocks and maroon cliffs everywhere. Some were shaped like bells, and others resembled church steeples. There were bur-gundy towers mixed in with pale green cacti and twisted mes-quite trees. I almost started to cry. My emotional numbing was gone—it was like the views of Sedona had uploaded a whole new range of emotions other than my normal three of mad, sad, and tired. I felt *alive* again. I had new revelations every day.

One was that depression is a totally inward experience. When I was depressed, I was unable to be objective and think outside myself.

I began working out again. After one of my training sessions, I met up with Lori, a nutritionist I worked with after I was wounded. She could see that I had changed and told me so. I told her about Dr. Beck, and I confided in her that I had nearly killed myself. She was quiet; then tears filled her eyes. "You would have hurt a lot of people, Mike." Her comment stunned me. It took me a while to comprehend the greater meaning of Lori's response to my confession, and how I was linked to both the problem and the solution. The veteran community is plagued by suicides. The grim reality is that to date we have lost far more veterans to suicide than we have to the wars in Iraq and Afghanistan combined. Because of this, experts have labeled the problem an epidemic. It seems strange to use the term *epidemic* to describe a condition like suicide.

But, depending on how you hear it, *epidemic* is being used as both a noun, to describe the widespread occurrence, and an adjective to explain its penetration into the veteran community. All epidemics must have a transmittal source, and this is where I fit in. Social epidemics are spread by social networks,* and veteran suicide is a social epidemic. It spreads because social networks are both influential and sympathetic. The veteran community is very closely connected and easily influenced by each other. Epidemics by their very nature must be able to go in any direction, and because of this they can end as fast as they start. It occurred to me after Lori's comment, that I would

---

* NA Christakis and JH Fowler, "The Spread of Obesity in a Large Social Network over 32 Years," *New England Journal of Medicine* 357, no. 4 (2007): 370–79, https://www.nejm.org/doi/full/10.1056/NEJMsa066082.

have hurt a lot of people, meant that I can move the epidemic in any direction based on my actions. My friend Lori knew this, as she'd worked with many of my warrior brothers and sisters who were struggling and barely holding on.

I often hear people ask, What is the Veteran Administration doing about the epidemic? And the answer is their best. The fact is, the VA couldn't fix me; I had to find my own treatment program. I was worn out and had tried so many things, I wouldn't have found it if Brenda and others I trusted and loved hadn't pushed me. Over the years, I have been trained so that I can always improve my situation, always. To do this, all I needed to do was move forward into the unknown, into the uncomfortable. Mr. Rogers had it right all along: "If you could only sense how important you are to the lives of those you meet; how important you can be to the people you may never even dream of..."

My Three-Strike Rule

My new role as jump master included jumping out of planes with the guys in sustained airborne training, managing the drop zones as the safety officer, doing personnel inspections, and delivering pre- and post-jump briefings. It was lots of work, but I loved it.

We would attempt to get in as many night jumps as possible. It was a process of packing chutes, loading up the plane, jumping, falling, deploying chutes, hitting the drop zone, and doing it all over again. Jumping out of a plane and falling at 120 miles per hour can be fun, but it will also wear you out. The key to jumping, like almost everything else in life, is to know how to relax, and then do it. The throw-out on a standard parachute is located on the bottom of the container, which required me to reach behind my back with my right arm, then grab and throw the pilot chute out to deploy the main canopy. I had done the maneuver well over two thousand times over the years; however, I had only jumped several times since being wounded. The bullets that shattered my right scapula at times caused muscle spasms that locked up my right arm, hand, and back. I have a personal three-strike rule: I allow myself three screwups, and after the third, I quit. It makes zero sense to tempt fate, especially when falling to earth at 120 miles per hour.

In my new instructor role, I had three cutaways while training with the guys. All three cutaways were from intense muscle spasms that kept me from using my right arm. My first main chute cutaway was more or less routine; I couldn't reach my chute to deploy it. So was the second. Both happened on jumps in Arizona. A few weeks later, I was in Arizona again for a jump, with only one strike remaining. I was falling in a peaceful arch over the night desert; I moved my right arm from out in front of me and began the simple motion of reaching behind my back when I felt my muscles lock up. My right arm and hand were useless. I immediately cut away and was able to deploy my reserve chute, but it was a hard opening and I felt a sharp pain in my chest that ran from my arm down to my thumb. I didn't know what had happened, but I knew it wasn't good. I managed to float to the ground and land on my reserve parachute. Strike three—I was done. I'd torn my pectoral muscle off the bone and needed to have it surgically repaired.

I dodged death after being shot twenty-seven times and blown up with a grenade. I'd had a brush with suicide, and now I'd just ripped my muscle off the bone after two previous cutaways—not to mention the six I'd had on the jump team years ago—all while attempting to deploy my parachute speeding toward the ground at 120 miles per hour. I've been seriously considering modifying the math on my three-strike rule formula to a more reduced one.

Unfortunately, my self-imposed rule also meant that I would need to resign as an air operations trainer, and I did. However, as my dumb luck would have it, my employer needed to fill another instructor role: close-quarters combat (CQC), Special Operations Urban Combat (SOUC) trainer. I was offered the job and I accepted. I got to stay with the guys, training the next generation of Navy SEALs in CQC and room clearing.

I had been one of the CQC trainers in my last platoon back in Iraq. Shortly after I was wounded, and partly because of what happened in the room that night, Naval Special Warfare revised some of the CQC training. We now have several new training methods. Ironically, my new job was to teach our SEALs how *not* to get in the same position I had. When I arrived at the training command, everyone already knew who I was and what had happened to me that night back in Iraq.

This new role is awesome. At forty-eight years old, after being all shot up, I'm still able to strap on heavy body armor and a helmet and go to work training the young guys the same way I did when I was a SEAL. Admiral McRaven better keep training—I'll be seeing him on the O-course.

Things are different now, because I'm different. On breaks and after work, I get a chance to talk with the guys. I offer honest answers to their questions, like *When was the last time you actually cried?* I tell them the truth—that I cry often, and sometimes it's spontaneous, because it takes a while for my experiences and their impact to catch up with my emotions. The guys share their ideas and fears with me because they feel safe. They feel safe because they trust me, and I trust them. Trusted relationships are essential, and they are what kept me alive.

I like to think that the training I provide is more like mentoring on how to navigate some of life's challenges than it is simply about navigating enemy-filled rooms. Strange as it may sound, being wounded was one of the best things that ever happened to me, in part because I can now use the knowledge gained from that experience—as well as my childhood—to help mentor, train, and protect the men doing this dangerous work on behalf of us all. The guys that I worked with at the Air, CQC, and SOUC cells became an integral part of my ongoing recovery. Although none of them are doctors, they delivered powerful medicine in the form of their positive attitudes and instantly making me feel part of the crew. I was with my brothers again. They are an amazing group of people doing a very dangerous job...A small community of trusted friends can be a lifesaver.

CHAPTER 20

Tattoos

My friend Mike Martin, a tattoo artist, was a team guy and a Vietnam veteran. He joined the Navy in 1968 and was an old-school Underwater Demolition Team (UDT) guy before going to BUD/S and graduating in class 50. After multiple tours in Vietnam, he came back from his war and exited the Navy in 1972, got married, and started a family. Then, in 1985, at thirty-six years old—after a thirteen-year break in service—he reenlisted in the Navy and did BUD/S all over again, graduating in class 138. Mike was a very influential guy and a mentor to many teammates. Mike had a few bullet hole tattoos covering the places where he had been shot in Vietnam. I thought it would be cool if Mike would do bullet hole tattoos to cover up my bullet hole scars. The tattoos are far more noticeable than the scars ever were. But the scars were created by my enemies, and the tattoos were my own doing. It was my own way of gaining a sense of agency over both the enemy and the wounds they'd inflicted. The tattoos simultaneously memorialize and eclipse those old wounds.

The ink that covers the scars gives me a sense of control, and they make the wounds seem far less serious. Mike Martin served as the founder and national president of the Frogmen Motorcycle Club. On May 30, 2019, my friend, Master Chief Mike Martin of SEAL Teams 1 and 3, passed from this world. He had just finished his last ride with the boys to the Vietnam Veterans Memorial. He was the real deal: a combat veteran, a straight-up warrior, and a great SEAL. It's very cool that I have some of Mike's work etched on me.

All Enemies

It's been over thirty years since that young, cocky, blond-haired, blue-eyed seventeen-year-old kid took an oath to protect and defend this nation from all enemies, foreign and domestic. These enemies were obscure back then. My remaining hair is now gray, and over the years I have fought both kinds of enemies.

The enemy I faced at home is the same one that many veterans face, an asymmetrical one brought on by trauma. This enemy was dangerous because it had infiltrated me and had been building up for years. The tentacles of trauma dragged me back to live in the past. My thoughts were hijacked; my mind was spinning. My condition, and the enemy, were held in place and then advanced by hormone imbalances, a poor diet, my genetics, childhood trauma, years of different antibiotic treatments, chronic inflammation, and microbiota–gut–brain axis dysfunction. To be fair, I did try all sorts of conventional medicine and modalities to treat my depression and the effects of PTSD. Mental health is very complicated, and unfortunately, none of the usual treatment programs for mental health disorders were able to address the underlying conditions or offer me long-term relief. It occurred to me later that fighting an asymmetrical enemy with conventional methods would never be truly successful. It was only when I turned to unconventional methods—or, as the conventional medical community calls it, *alternative treatment*—did I find the cure for my depression.

In his *New York Times* bestselling book *The Body Keeps the Score*, author Bessel van der Kolk writes: "Trauma remains the greatest threat to our public health...We seem too embarrassed to mount a massive effort to help children and adults learn to deal with the fear, rage and collapse, the predictable consequences of having been traumatized."

I believe that part of our avoidance and embarrassment is due to the stigma of depression as being solely a *mental* illness. Most still believe that these are wholly psychological conditions, when in fact they are both mental *and* physical. Bessel van der Kolk, MD, first started studying trauma in the early 1970s with a group of Vietnam veterans. His life's work has been dedicated to studying the effects of trauma on individuals and society. He goes on to say:

> Untreated trauma is more expensive than cancer or heart disease: lost work, unemployment, drug addiction, hospitalization, chronic illness, family violence, two and a half million people in jail, and all those kids who have parents in jail. It's a vast public health issue, and all of it interferes with learning and with being productive and engaging. The ideal person is a tax-paying member of society. We pay something so we can build roads, theaters, and hospitals, etc. Many traumatized people grow up to be sick. So, resources are used for drug rehabilitation, chronic illness, unemployment, and

prisons. All terrible ways to spend too few resources. Show me a person in jail who has not been traumatized. Eighty percent of prisoners in California have spent time in the foster care system. They were unwanted and did not have a steady caregiver. These are huge things that are continuously pushed off the radar screen. Drug addiction is a function of child abuse. It's possible to become a drug addict without child abuse, but it's very hard.

I believe that Dr. van der Kolk is spot-on.

CHAPTER 21

Personal Revolution: Resiliency Skills and Tools

It may seem strange but being shot twenty-seven times, then having a grenade blow up next to me was one of the best things that had ever happened to me. It was the start of a personal revolution that continues today and hopefully will go on until I take my last breath. I say *revolution* rather than *evolution*. As a result of my experience, I have tossed out and/or abandoned every bias, relationship, belief, and dogma that has blocked my self-awareness and joy. A revolution is not a static event set in time; it's a set of ideas that are tested every day. All revolutions begin as personal ones, erupting internally, triggered by a single idea before they manifest externally in actions. The struggle between old ideas and new ones, good and evil, takes place inside of us all each day.

My journey toward joy and self-awareness has been a hard-fought one. It has required more courage, honesty, and humility than I thought I had in me. It has been a series of trials and errors and definitely not a straight line. To put this into perspective, this journey has been far more difficult than BUD/S training or working as a Navy SEAL. There were times when I thought that my depression would never end, that the white noise buzzing in my head would never shut off, that I would never love or trust anyone again, and—worst of all—that I would never find peace.

I burned through a number of different therapists. Some were good, but most didn't have what I needed to help me understand how the traumas of my childhood shaped me as a person, and how those same traumas make some of my behaviors predictable. At times, I had to be pushed into seeing therapists and doctors by people who loved and cared about me. I don't know if I can ever thank these people enough for not giving up on me when I was so rude and resistant toward them.

I say all of this so you know that, at least for me, there has been no magic pill, quick fix, or one-size-fits-all solution to finding peace and joy in my life. These things have come to me slowly over the past decade as I grew in self-awareness and courage. I suspect your personal peace, if that's what you're searching for, may be gained much the same way.

Trauma is indiscriminate and for many of us unavoidable. While my childhood was a little rough, it was tame compared to what others have experienced. As I've mentioned before, being wounded turned out to be one of the best things that ever happened to me. I would put it up there as being as transformational as the birth of my daughters. It led me on an incredible, unlikely journey of recovery and self-discovery. Turns out I checked almost every trauma box: childhood trauma, long-term exposure to stress and violence, physical trauma, bouts of infection resolved with countless antibiotics that led to bad gut flora, which led to a deep depression.

All of these factors—combined with other conditions—drove me to consider suicide. Suicide is a condition of hopelessness, and I have come to learn that the cure for hopelessness is the right relationships in your life. My old boss, Scott; my wife, Brenda; my nurse friend who met me at the emergency room; Dr. Beck; my SEAL brothers; and my buddy Adam, who on one of my worst days of my life dropped everything and stayed by my side to help get me through the next second, minute, and hour. There are so many others who have loved me more than I love myself. They saw things in me that I couldn't, and some of those things are still hard for me to see. They didn't look past my many faults but loved me for them. They saw only my strengths and potential. They all came into my life at the perfect time. Based on the adverse childhood experience study, my family history, getting wounded, and the grim number of veteran suicides, I guess you could say that my downward spiral was predictable.

That's what makes my recovery so impressive. I have way more stress and uncertainty in my life today than I ever did in the SEAL teams or when I was suicidal. The difference is that now I have a new resiliency portfolio of people, tools, and skills that allows me to effectively manage stress almost effortlessly. While I do have bad days, and very bad days, they don't control me or impact my outlook on life. I'm also keenly aware that most of my troubles are self-inflicted. If you are honest with yourself, you may find that the same is true in your own life.

Adversity is either a privilege or a tragedy, depending on how you respond to it. Choosing to be a victim of the events and circumstances in my life would be the real tragedy. What if we all viewed adversity as an opportunity for personal growth, to define our life's purpose, and to help others? The reality is that we can, but we can't do any of these things as victims. If I am to evolve, which is my life's mission, I can't be a victim. Even if my problems are the result of someone else's actions, I've found it easier to fix it myself than to rely on the perpetrator to repair the damage.

Strong and Flexible

I'm a salty old sailor now, and I love my Navy and her ships. The USS *Constitution* is the oldest commissioned warship in the U.S. Navy. She earned her nickname "Old Ironside" in a legendary sea battle during the War of 1812. It was near six o'clock on the evening of August 19, 1812, when the British frigate HMS *Guerrière* maneuvered twenty-five yards alongside the USS *Constitution*. The American ship fired first and rocked the HMS *Guerrière* with a full volley of cannon fire directly into her side. The British ship responded with a volley from her guns. As the metal balls slammed into the side of the *Constitution*, the enemy crew watched in amazement as each of its eighteen-pound iron cannonballs bounced harmlessly off the *Constitution*'s twenty-four-inch, triple-layered hull. Legend has it that one of the British sailors shouted, "Her sides are made of iron!" Thus, the nickname "Old Ironsides."

A host of naval craftsmen from different parts of the young nation added their unique experiences to that ship. The rock-hard, triple-layered hull of the *Constitution* was made of white and live oak, then sheathed in copper forged by none other than Paul Revere. Nearly 150,000 treenails, wooden pegs made of steel-like black locust wood, were used to pin the ship's hull together. Her beams and decks were made of longleaf pine, a flexible, durable wood harvested from South Carolina. The ship's rigging components were made of a lignum vitae, one of the hardiest, heaviest woods in the world that readily sinks in water. The *Constitution's* masts were made of Eastern white pine. Eastern pines flourished along America's Northeastern coast, largely because they bend with the violent winds generated by seasonal nor'easters—the regional winter storms that pound the coast. The more rigid trees in this region snapped or were uprooted by the stress of the nor'easter's winds. The rake of the *Constitution's* masts are at such an angle that when the wind furls her enormous 47,710 square feet of sails, her giant eastern white pine masts bend forward, driving the massive 44-gun, 304-foot-long, 2,200-ton vessel through the ocean at an impressive thirteen knots, or near fifteen miles per hour. The ability of the *Constitution's* masts to bend and not break keeps the masts rooted on her deck and it's what made the ship one of the fastest on the sea.

The combination of strength and flexibility is what accounts for the USS *Constitution's* legendary resiliency and longevity. Her naval architects and shipbuilders knew which parts of the ship to make strong in order to withstand the damage of war and the elements. They also knew which parts to make flexible in order to create durability and increase speed by absorbing the stress of the wind.

We are all unique ships created by a combination of nature, nurture, experiences, and relationships. My childhood's perfect wounds made me strong in all the right places and flexible in others. The greatest accomplishments of my life have come as a result of my childhood experiences. My father, the SEAL teams, and many others helped to build my ship. My father made a part of me as hard as iron and another part of me flexible and able to absorb the damage of war and the tolls of my life.

Knowing which parts to make rigid and which ones to make flexible comes by way of experience, knowledge, and applied wisdom. My ongoing responsibility is to transform my experiences and knowledge into assets and to use them to benefit others. Over the years, I have rebuilt my ship to become more flexible in some areas and rigid in others. This has helped me to sail through some of life's more violent storms and dangerous battles. The irony of the ship's name is not lost on me:

Con·sti·tu·tion; noun: the composition of something.

My life has been a nonstop adventure, one filled with dumb luck and perfect wounds. You could describe my dumb luck as grace, which I once heard defined as "anything that arrives for you without warning and without having to be earned." My youngest daughter's middle name is Grace, and in the most desperate times of my life, when my violent death seemed unavoidable, like it did the night in that room in the compound, my heart and mind were suddenly and without warning filled with the thoughts of my girls. I never asked them for help, and thus, in a sense it seems unearned. Their grace came to me without warning, filled me, and saved me.

After everything that I have come through, I'm grateful. I think that gratitude and service are inseparable. The more I serve, the more grateful I feel that I can still serve and care for my family, my warrior brothers and sisters, and to continue to be of service to all of you. These days I spend my free time hunting for perfect surf and spending time with great friends. I set up a nonprofit to help shorten the distance to recovery from trauma and depression. We join with people who truly want to help themselves. We offer these adventurous souls a community of the right relationships and a portfolio of resiliency skills and tools. To learn more, visit www.warriortribe.org.

Joseph Clark Schwedler

It comes in waves now and again. There's an overwhelming feeling of disbelief that gives way to frustration; then my eyes usually well up. It's been going on for years now. I have lost so many people; it takes a toll.

Clark was the kind of man you want your son to grow up to be. He was smart, driven, had a great sense of humor, was tough but thoughtful, and responsible. He was a born leader and he made us all better people. After missions, we'd all be tired, but Clarkie would be working out, so we'd work out too. He was like a Swiss Army knife: he was our navigator, our intel-collections guy, a team leader, sensitive site exploitation officer, and one of our Iraqi Army combat advisors. He picked up everything fast and became great at whatever he did.

Clark's dream was to be a Navy SEAL. He was a Midwestern kid from Crystal Falls, a northern Michigan town of 1,469 people. He was his senior class president, played high school football and basketball, and ran track. He did two years at Michigan State and joined the rowing team. Knowing Clarkie, he did it because the workouts were grueling, and he wanted to stay in shape. He followed his heart, abandoned college, and enlisted in the Navy to fulfill his dream of becoming a SEAL.

Clarkie got to live his dream and did what he loved to do. Every time I saw him, he had a smile on his face. What gives me peace is knowing that if I died doing my job as a SEAL, I would have no regrets. I know Clarkie felt the same way.

For those of us who have lost friends and family members in this war, the losses connect us; while we may be strangers, we know each other well. There is a surprising comfort in being together in this painful club. We don't have words to describe the depth of our grief, but we don't need them because we can feel each other's sorrow.

There's a saying: "Time heals all wounds." It doesn't—it only makes them slightly less painful. I may again meet up with Clarkie on the other side of this life, and I'm looking forward to it.

Acknowledgments

I'm grateful for all those who made me the person I am today. I appreciate every person who gave me an experience that influenced my growth. I have been guided by people who caused me trauma and others who showed me love. You are the yin and yang in my life that made me more balanced.

Thank you to the ones who hurt me and forced me to find the path on my own.

Thank you to the ones who provided a helping hand and nurturing that I needed, even when I refused it. It was no coincidence that you were all there right when you were supposed to, and whether you're known to me now or not, I will see you all one day.

About the Authors

Douglas "Mike" Day was born in New Jersey and moved to Virginia Beach in grade school. He grew up in a chaotic home and endured periods of homelessness. At seventeen he enlisted in the Navy.

Senior Chief Petty Officer Mike Day proudly served twenty-one years and three months as a U.S. Navy SEAL. He is a skilled leader with a unique ability to bring out the best in others. As a platoon leader, he was responsible for the professional development of his SEAL team.

Mike is an expert at intelligence gathering and tactical operations, including open- and closed-water SCUBA diving, free-falling and static-line parachuting, helicopter rope suspension techniques, breaching, small arms, and explosives. He is a free-fall and static line Jumpmaster and his career included three years as a member of the Navy's Elite Leap Frogs skydiving team. He has deployed to Kosovo, the Philippines, and multiple combat deployments to the Middle East.

On what would be his final combat mission as a Navy SEAL, Mike was shot at close range by four enemy fighters and absorbed a grenade blast. Despite being wounded, Mike was able to neutralize all four enemy combatants, secure two prisoners, rescue six women and children, and evacuate to an awaiting helicopter.

Mike's greatest work came after his retirement when he led over three hundred of his fellow warriors as a Special Operations Command Wounded Warrior Advocate. Mike continues to lead and train other military special operations personnel and law enforcement professionals as a tactical training instructor. Mike is the founder of Warrior Tribe, a nonprofit organization that provides resiliency education for young people, veterans, and trauma survivors. Mike speaks at corporations and schools on the power of the human connection and developing resiliency skills. He is a frequent guest speaker on behalf of the Navy SEAL Foundation and other organizations.

Mike's military awards include the Navy Cross; two Bronze Stars, one with Valor; a Purple Heart; and a number of other commendations. His community service awards include the 2019 Heirs of the Republic, the Freedom Fighter award, and the 2008 Jewish Institute for National Security Affairs award.

Robert Vera's first book, *A Warrior's Faith* (Thomas Nelson, March 2015), became a bestseller and earned the publishing industry's 2016 Illumination Silver Medal Award for Best Memoir.

Robert was born and raised in Boston, Massachusetts, and earned a bachelor's degree in political science from Boston College. Prior to his writing career, he worked as a staff assistant to a United States senator, where he managed military and veteran constituent services. He transitioned from government into investment banking then founded a successful software company.

Robert serves as Honorary Commander of the 161st Air Force National Guard Squadron, he is a board member of Friends of Freedom, and is the founder of The Institute for

Transformation, a servant leadership training organization. Robert is a mentor to a group of veterans and leads warriors on an annual expedition across the Grand Canyon. He is an active athlete and has completed multiple Ironman Triathlons.

Robert is married with children and lives in Phoenix, Arizona, where he works as a professional author and speaker.